Peacock.

Singapore 56.

THROUGH THE AGES

VOL. I
FROM THE BEGINNING TO THE REFORMATION

"Picture Post"

CORONATION OF BALDWIN III AS KING OF JERUSALEM
From a late 15th-century MS. "Conquête de Jérusalem"

THROUGH THE AGES

*The Story of the
Christian Church*

VOL. I
FROM THE BEGINNING TO
THE REFORMATION

by

the late FRANCIS E. BARKER, M.A.

With a Foreword by
THE RIGHT REV.
THE LORD BISHOP OF WINCHESTER

Published for
THE CHURCH ASSEMBLY CHILDREN'S COUNCIL
by
THE CHURCH INFORMATION BOARD
Church House, Westminster, S.W.1

First published 1955

Made and printed in Great Britain by
William Clowes and Sons, Limited, London and Beccles

Foreword

The author of this book was a country parson who spent the last twenty-three years of his ministry in the diocese of Winchester. He died this year, to our great loss, after a long struggle with ill-health and before he could see the publication of his work. At first he had intended nothing more ambitious than a series of lesson notes, but his plan grew wider as time passed, though he still had in mind as his primary purpose the provision of a book which would help the teachers of older boys and girls and which some at least of those boys and girls might read for themselves.

I believe he has succeeded not only in fulfilling this purpose but in writing a work which very many others will do well to read. He was a man devoted to true religion and sound learning; his reading of the best books, old and new, was wide and discriminating; he had a wise and tolerant judgement. All this comes out clearly in his book. So too does the impression of a singularly attractive character, and an understanding sympathy springing from his own experience. I hope and believe that this admirable book will bring to those who read it a living sense of the greatness and fascination of its subject.

ALWYN WINTON:

June, 1955

Contents

VOLUME I

vii

Contents

Contents

List of Illustrations

VOLUME I

List of Illustrations

VOLUME II

Preface

These chapters are meant primarily, though not exclusively, to furnish material and background for teachers of older Church seniors, who wish to help them acquire some knowledge of the history of the Christian Church of which they are members. Others who are not teachers may find in them a kind of bird's-eye view of the past which is not without relevance to the present. These chapters could also be used as a class book by older children themselves. Their writing arose out of a request which came to me, and which I felt I could not refuse, after I had drawn up a Church History syllabus as a member of a committee which met under the aegis of the Children's Council of the Church of England Council for Education. I should not otherwise have had the temerity to embark upon so comprehensive a project, making considerable demands, which for one reason or another has taken a long time to complete.

If there is some unevenness of treatment, this is not, I think, due in the main to the fact that the writing of the book was sometimes interrupted by a matter of many months. It is due much more to the first draft of the chapters down to the Middle Ages having been written after their contents had been tried out in an actual class, whereas the rest of the book, except for bits here and there, has not been taught in class. Several of the later chapters formed the basis of talks to Sunday school teachers at a Summer School. Further, from the Reformation onwards, the history has been dealt with somewhat more fully; it seemed very undesirable to leave too many and too obvious gaps, such as had to be left, inevitably, at the earlier stages.

The class with which I tried out the earlier part of this book consisted of about a dozen boys and girls drawn from my two adjacent country parishes. They ranged in age from fairly young seniors to one or two of about sixteen who had left school. Only one member attended a Grammar School, though another boy was shortly afterwards transferred to the Winchester School of Art. I should not have believed that these boys and girls would have appreciated Church History in the way that they obviously did, if I had not tried the experiment. But it is by no means easy to devise suitable activities. Note-books were kept, members usually suggesting at the end what might be entered in them, and the filling in of outline maps was liked. A few film-strips were shown. Some of the exercises given at the end of this book were actually worked, but the suggested activities should be regarded merely as suggestions thrown out in the hope that other teachers may devise better ones.

The purpose which these chapters attempt to serve sufficiently explains the kind of illustrative matter which is used, and why in a few places an excursion is made a little outside the usual field of Church History. Religion after all touches life at many points, and in teaching our children this must always be borne in mind. Inevitably my own particular interests were bound to dictate the nature of the excursions made.

At a number of places I have used local illustrations, mostly drawn from my present parishes of Hinton Ampner and Bramdean, a few miles out of Winchester. This does not mean that there is anything very special about them, although the fact that the estate of "Hentone" was for some centuries attached to the Almonry of the Cathedral Monastery of St Swithun has meant that more records relating to the parish survive from the late Middle Ages than is the case with many parishes—my other parish of Bramdean, for example. I have drawn on what I had available in the hope that others will do the same. The stones of our old parish churches are rich in history, and from their registers alone, and perhaps, if they have been preserved, churchwardens' account books, overseers' books, Vestry minute books, much that is of interest can be gleaned. As for our old churches, I like to recall the words of Mr Edmund Blunden, in his *Cricket Country*: "All the contraries are at home here. An old church is like a big family, at a perpetual reunion; and its fascination comes largely from its eccentricities of detail and its harmonizing central spirit."

As the work proceeded I became conscious of a growing contraction, which brought home in a new way what a divided Christendom means. To begin with, Christendom became contracted—never wholly but inevitably largely—to Western Christendom. An interest, which I have had from student days, in the Orthodox Church, probably saved me from greater contraction. Then, with the Reformation, supervened yet further contraction. The main stream followed from this point is naturally the Anglican, but I have tried never to lose sight of the other streams, whether Catholic or Protestant, and I hope that I have been fair in what I have said about them. If the choice has been dictated partly by my own limitations of knowledge, as well as by limitations of space, the Church of England is the church of my baptism and ordination, the only church which I know at first hand. In the account of the history of the post-Reformation Anglican church I have tried not to be unduly tendentious, but to present fairly points of view that are not my own, and to admit quite frankly differences of opinion among members of the Anglican communion where such in fact exist.

In a work of this character one's debt to other writers must be very great. This is partly acknowledged in footnotes and by the inclusion of a bibliography; but so much must go un-acknowledged. It has been possible to make a few alterations and additions at a late stage, which it is hoped has brought the recent history reasonably up to date. It has not been possible to make use of Dr Moorman's *A History of the Church in England*, published late in 1953, but it is included in the bibliography since it is likely to become and remain for a long time the standard book on its subject. Considerable use was made of Professor J. E. (now Sir John) Neale's *Elizabeth I and her Parliaments*. Just how strong the Puritan party was in Parliament and within the Church of England, and how much all who believe that "the middle way" was the right way stand in the Queen's debt, any reader of this important book will have brought home to him.

It remains to make a few further acknowledgements. I have to express my thanks to those who have made various suggestions, some of them to the great improvement of the book, or who have helped in other ways.

The extracts from the registers of St Simon and St Jude's Church, Bramdean, were kindly photographed for me by Mr R. H. Chatterton, of Bramdean. One of them invites one word as a sort of postscript. When the 250th anniversary of the S.P.G. was being celebrated, a distinguished Jamaican priest, four generations removed from slavery, preached at Bramdean church in the morning and talked to the children in the afternoon. As we entered by the lych gate, he gathered a small Sunday school child into his arms and walked into church with her, passing the font at which had once been baptized "Sara, alias Benjamin Hope", from the Colony of Sierra Leone.

FRANCIS E. BARKER

Hinton Ampner Rectory,
Alresford,
Hampshire.

PUBLISHER'S NOTE

At the time of his sudden death, it was the author's intention to add to the preface an expression of thanks to Canon E. F. Carpenter of Westminster and Canon H. W. Dobson, Honorary Editorial Secretary of the Children's Council, for kindly reading the typescript and making many valuable suggestions; and to the latter in addition for securing the illustrations and seeing the book through the press. Mr. Barker himself corrected the first proofs of his book but did not live to see it in its final form.

1

The Faith Spreads

Our subject is the story of the Christian Church from Pentecost
to the present. Even if we thought of the Church simply as a
human institution—as John Locke called it, in his famous
Letter on Toleration (1689), "a voluntary society of men, joining
themselves together of their own accord, in order to the public
worshipping of God, in such a manner as they judge acceptable
to Him, and effectual to the salvation of souls"—it would
still be helpful to know by what stages it had come to be as it
now is, and how Christians down the ages had worshipped God
and lived their lives. But is this an adequate definition? Something, surely, has been left out. No Christian of New Testament
times would have thought of the Church in this way. For
primitive Christianity the Church was something not made by
man but given by God—given by Him to man, called into being
by God Himself to be the instrument and organ of Christ's
redemptive work in the world. For the early Christian, as for
St Paul, it was the Body of which Christ is the Head. Christians
to-day are members of the same Body, the Body which in the
early days gave us the Gospels, gave us the New Testament, and
before that met in the Upper Room at Jerusalem.

That first community was very small and very simple, the
Twelve and a few others, a tiny community. Now the Church is
world-wide. It is true that too much must not be made of this,
for there are parts of the world where Christians are very thinly
scattered and where at the present time the Church is maintain-
ing no more than a precarious foothold, and places where it is
not found at all. But it *is* a world-wide community. Here
obviously we see a development; but development implies continuity. Even at the Reformation, when most reformed Churches
showed a disposition to break with the past, the Church of
England preserved—it may seem almost by a miracle—the
historic continuity of its ministry, a continuity which it quickly
came to value. Its aim was to remedy abuses and to get back,
so far as was possible, to the teaching and practice of the early

1

ages. Its ideal came to be the Church of the first four centuries. Yet those early centuries themselves saw far-reaching developments. We shall need to know something at least about them if we are to understand what happened at the Reformation, and we shall need to know what took place then if we are to be intelligent members of the Church of Christ, and of our own Anglican communion, at the present day.

It is not very likely that, if we are Anglicans, we shall imagine that the Church of Christ comprises none but Anglicans. What is much more probable is that we shall so largely confine our outlook to our own communion, from the Reformation onwards, that for practical purposes it occupies almost our whole field of vision. This is inevitable, perhaps; but that only makes it all the more necessary to remind ourselves at the outset of its smallness. But size is not everything. "Its significance is derived not from its size, but from its genius. 'It hath been the wisdom of the Church of England,' says the Preface to the Prayer Book, 'ever since the first compiling of her Public Liturgy, to keep the mean between the two extremes.' It is the combination of the Protestant and Catholic factors in the same body which gives the Church of England its peculiar quality. It is conscious of both sides of the shield simultaneously. It is therefore in a favourable position for appreciating both the Catholic and the Protestant Churches, and even speaking to them both at the same time."[1]

The Roman Catholic Church is to-day the largest and strongest Christian communion. At least half the Christians in the world look to the Pope as their head. This will help to explain why, when the Pope speaks to the world on some subject of importance to all Christians, his words are listened to by members of all Christian Churches and of none. In part it may also explain why, among all Christian bodies, the Roman Catholic Church arouses the fiercest opposition in totalitarian countries. But here the principal factor is that Rome is herself political and totalitarian. To see how this came about, how the Papacy arose and also some of the changes through which it passed, will not fail to throw light on the present. Again, why the Eastern Orthodox Church finds it more easily possible to come to terms with, and exist in, a non-Christian environment, may also become clear from her history. She learnt, long ago, to exist under such conditions. In any case, we are reminded of a stream of Christianity which most English people, though never

[1] G. K. A. Bell: *Christian Unity*, p. 10.

2

for very long the Church of England itself, tend to forget. The non-episcopal communions are always with us. In some European countries they contain the bulk of the Christian population; and, as with Rome and Eastern Orthodoxy, their leading confessions have more adherents throughout the world than have the churches which look to Canterbury. What are the differences and what are the points in common between other Christian communions and ourselves?

THE CHRISTIAN PAST

These are in all conscience matters of practical concern, and, to go back to our quotation from the Bishop of Chichester, the Anglican ought to be peculiarly well placed to understand the position of those, on both sides, from whom in certain matters he differs. One thing the Anglican of to-day will not do—he will not imagine that Christian history between the early centuries and the Reformation is no concern of his. As well believe, with the complacent self-assurance of the eighteenth century, that the entire experience of the past can be written off! The Church of England is heir to a long Christian tradition, to the whole of the Christian past.

And what a different story the secular historian would have to tell if there were no Christian past! Professor Butterfield has said: "The ordinary historian, when he comes, shall we say, to the year 1800 does not think to point out to his readers that in this year, still, as in so many previous years, thousands and thousands of priests and ministers were preaching the Gospel week in and week out, constantly reminding the farmer and the shopkeeper of charity and humility, persuading them to think for a moment about the great issues of life, and inducing them to confess their sins. Yet this was a phenomenon calculated greatly to alter the quality of life and the very texture of human history; and it has been the standing work of the Church throughout the ages—even under the worst of popes here was a light that never went out. . . . It is impossible to measure the difference that ordinary Christian piety has made in the last two thousand years of European history." [1] No more than the ordinary historian can we break into our narrative to point this out; but it will come out from time to time, and all the time it will be there—a vital factor in the story.

[1] H. Butterfield: *Christianity and History*, p. 131.

THE KINGDOM IN THE MAKING

Our Lord, on the night before the Crucifixion, prayed "that they all may be one" (cf. Jn. 17. 11 and 20–23). There is no doubt that the divisions of Christendom make non-Christians less ready to believe that Christianity is true, and weaken the Church as a force in the world ranged against the forces of evil. We are brought face to face with something which we have to remember all the time, that the Christian not only lives in a fallen world—a world in which evil persists—but is part and parcel of it. The grace bestowed in baptism does not remove the "kink" in our nature which theologians call "original sin". The Church between Pentecost and the end of the world is not unlike Israel of old, journeying "in the wilderness . . . toward the sunrising" (Num. 21. 11)—a Church still struggling, still on the way, not yet arrived at the Promised Land. Call it the Church in the wilderness; or better still, the Kingdom of God in the making.

We ought not to be very surprised to find Christians behaving badly, sometimes very badly. They were just not being Christian enough. We are children, not puppets. God will not force us to behave like Christians, though He gives us all the means we need to enable us to do so. It is because, on its human side, the Church consists of fallen, though redeemed, human beings, that we find sin making such constant inroads even in the Church itself. Thus, while we can give plausible reasons why schisms have occurred within the Christian Body, whether in the fifth century or the sixteenth, or in the centuries between, it really comes back to our living in a sinful world. Occasionally in these pages the most sorry doings by professing Christians have had to be recorded. We must not shut our eyes to them nor make too much of them. Happily we shall also discover what great things have been done by those who have been wholly devoted to Christ and have let His Spirit dominate their lives— indeed, are being done in our own day.

"BEGINNING FROM JERUSALEM"

When we consider the rapid spread of the Christian faith in the early years of Christianity, two external factors have to be remembered. First, that within the Roman Empire communications were comparatively easy. You could travel from end to end of the Empire without being stopped at a frontier, and you could travel on good roads, well policed and therefore reasonably safe. Communications were easier than they had ever been before or than they were to be for many a century after Rome's decline. And people did move about; there were constant comings and goings between Palestine and Asia Minor, between Ephesus and Corinth and Rome. There is an inscription mentioning a native of Bithynia who taught Greek at York before A.D. 70. And that brings us to the second external factor—the use of the *Koine* Greek by most of the townsfolk all around the Mediterranean seaboard. Anyone speaking Greek could get a hearing in Southern Gaul, in Italy—where the Roman Church was Greek-speaking until the third century—at Tarsus or Alexandria or Jerusalem. It is more than likely that our Lord Himself spoke Greek as well as Aramaic. But in any case the fact that the Gospel could be preached, and the Gospels written, in a language which so large a part of the civilized world understood was not without its effect.

In *The Groundwork of the Gospels* the late R. O. P. Taylor linked this external preparation for the Gospel with the preparation that had come through the native teachers of Israel and the facts of Israel's history. It is impossible, he says, "to view the whole as a mere chapter of accidents. A single purpose runs through it all. And the purpose remains clear at the culminating stage. Israel was now spread over the whole civilized world, and was speaking a language which the whole world understood. And Galilee, the cradle of the Gospel, had become a highway along which the world, in all its variety, moved incessantly to and fro. At home and abroad, the men of Galilee, as of all Jewry, having inherited all that the great civilizations could teach, as well as the knowledge, specially given to them, of the one God, were in a position to grasp, to teach and to circulate the religion which was the consummation of all religions."[1]

Our Lord, before His ascension, gave a commission to His disciples. "Ye shall receive power, when the Holy Ghost is come upon you: and ye shall be my witnesses both in Jerusalem, and in all Judaea and Samaria, and unto the uttermost part of the earth." St Luke, who records this in the opening chapter of the Acts of the Apostles (verse 8), in the concluding chapter tells of the proclamation of the Gospel at the very centre of the Roman world. St Paul was a prisoner, but the Gospel was being proclaimed in Rome. The last two verses indeed are the climax of the whole book: "And he abode two whole years

[1] P. xii.

in his own hired dwelling, and received all that went in unto
him, preaching the kingdom of God, and teaching the things
concerning the Lord Jesus Christ with all boldness, none forbidding him." The Gospel was on its way to reaching the uttermost part of the earth.

The progress of the Church can be seen if we mark off the
Acts of the Apostles into six sections, with a concluding verse
between each of the sections. If these concluding verses (omitted
in the table below) are referred to, it will be seen that they have
something in common—they each indicate a new stage of growth
and development.

1. 1. 1–6. 6.   Jerusalem.
2. 6. 8–9. 30.   Palestine.
3. 9. 32–12. 23. Antioch.
4. 12. 25–16. 4. Asia Minor.
5. 16. 6–19. 19. Europe (Macedonia, Achaia).
6. 19. 21–end.   Rome.

In Jerusalem it is obvious that the Faith at first won considerable acceptance: 1. 15—120 adherents; 2. 41—3,000; 4. 4—5,000;
5. 14—"multitudes both of men and women". The verse which
concludes this section tells us that "a great company of the
priests (i.e. the Temple priests) were obedient to the faith".
The serious Jewish rejection of Christianity seems to have begun when St Stephen made it clear that Christianity was something which would supersede Judaism, and was not just a
school within it. The scattering abroad of disciples on account
of the persecution which followed Stephen's death had, however, important consequences, and one was that men of Cyprus
and Cyrene preached at Antioch to Greeks, i.e. Gentiles, as
well as to Jews (Acts 11. 19, 20). (There is little doubt that R.V.
"Greeks", rather than A.V. "Grecians"—Greek-speaking
Jews—is the correct reading.) The preaching may have preceded that of St Peter to the household of Cornelius (Acts 10)
but in any case there is nothing to make us suppose that these
men of Cyprus and Cyrene were not just ordinary Christians.
We should never forget what the Church has owed to the zeal
and witness of the ordinary Christian. If the proclaiming of the
Good News and the first gathering together of disciples had
been left to the Twelve, or to St Paul, or to those others who in
the New Testament are called Apostles—such men as Barnabas,
Silas, Andronicus and Junias, all of whom may have received

a commission direct from the risen Jesus,[1] as had St Paul—the Faith could never have spread as it did. With the Church at Antioch, however, St Peter as well as St Paul and St Barnabas was associated, and there is something to be said for the tradition which makes St Luke, the writer of the third Gospel and the Acts, an Antiochene. It was the third city of the Roman world, and "the disciples were called Christians first in Antioch" (Acts 11. 26).

Acts 19. 20, although coming in a chapter wholly devoted to St Paul at Ephesus, is a good connecting link, because verse 21 looks forward to a visit to Rome. When at last the Apostle did land in Italy, at Puteoli, on the Bay of Naples, he found brethren there; and later brethren from Rome met him on his way to the city (Acts 28. 14, 15). He was not the first to plant the Church in Rome, nor, is there any reason to think, was St Peter. The tradition that both Apostles suffered martyrdom at Rome, firmly established in the second century, need not be doubted.

THE TWELVE

It was never St Luke's intention to write in the Acts about all the Apostles, but in the early chapters he tells us a good deal about St Peter: his preaching in the earliest days, his visit with St John to Samaria, his activities in a few Palestinian towns. From Gal. 2. 11 we know that he was at Antioch (where the church was later to claim him as its first bishop), and he was known to the Church at Corinth (1 Cor. 1. 12). It is very likely that he had visited the provinces, in northern and western Asia Minor, which are mentioned in the opening verse of 1 Peter. He can hardly have been long at Rome, and was probably put to death by Nero not long after St Paul.

We are told a little in the Acts about St John in the early days at Jerusalem, and chapter 12 tells us of the martyrdom of his brother, St James. This must have been between A.D. 41 and 44. But St John, if we are to believe Irenaeus (c. A.D. 180), lived on at Ephesus to extreme old age, dying during the reign of Trajan (A.D. 96–117). This has been questioned, but on no very good grounds. Where we are on much less secure ground is when we come to traditions about the rest of the Twelve. We will think for a moment about four of them whom tradition connects with the East.

[1] This is suggested by Dr A. M. Farrer in *The Apostolic Ministry*, ed. K. E. Kirk, Essay 3.

"TO INDIA, TO ST THOMAS"

Pilgrims from the East were present in Jerusalem on the Day of Pentecost; they would at least carry tidings of the events of that day to their homes. Further, we should notice that in the Middle East in the early Christian centuries Syriac was largely spoken; but this was a cognate language to Aramaic, and any Aramaic-speaking Palestinian Christian would have found little or no language difficulty in preaching the Gospel as far east as Mesopotamia. If many Palestinians also spoke Greek, Aramaic was with most the language of the hearth and home.

Centuries later, in A.D. 1296, there was a persecution of Christians by Moslems in Mesopotamia and many churches were destroyed. An Armenian bishop, Stephen, in whose lifetime this happened, says that the monastery in which reposed the mortal remains of St Thaddeus was ruined: this was probably at Dadi Vank, where the church was dedicated to St Thaddeus.[1] Thaddeus is the Jude of St Simon and St Jude—Matthew and Mark both call him Thaddeus. The Simon of St Simon and St Jude was by tradition sawn asunder in Persia. If there is *some* truth behind these accounts and traditions, both Apostles travelled east, as it is reasonably certain did St Bartholomew and St Thomas.

About A.D. 180, Pantaenus, a native of Sicily and afterwards famous as a teacher at Alexandria, went to "India", and found there a copy of a Hebrew version of St Matthew's Gospel, which it was said had been handed down from Christians converted by St Bartholomew. If this was so, then St Bartholomew had probably himself been to a locality which a fourth century writer—Eusebius—could call "India". Unfortunately the name was very loosely applied, and was sometimes used for Southern Arabia, which was on the way to India. Merchants visited India by crossing the Indian Ocean to the mouth of the Indus. Bartholomew, if he did not get to India, can quite well have got to Arabia.

But the ancient Christian Church of Malabar, in southern India, claims that St Thomas was its founder, in A.D. 52, and what tradition says about his activities is supported by facts otherwise known relating to persons and places in the India of that day. Scholars of repute cautiously accept the claim—but others of equal repute reject it. A Christian Church was in any case established in India in comparatively early days. Our own

[1] Cf. L. E. Browne: *The Eclipse of Christianity in Asia*, p. 165.

King Alfred, many years later, sent gifts by a bishop of Sherborne as a thankoffering to Rome, and "to India, to St Thomas". The bishop reached the Malabar coast, offered the gifts, and brought back presents of jewels and pepper.

AFRICA AND HOME

The native Coptic Church of Egypt claims St Mark as its founder and says that he was martyred by followers of the god Serapis, who dragged him bound in a procession through the streets of Alexandria till he died. The curious thing is, however, that although Alexandria by the end of the second century had produced a number of famous writers, none of them mention Mark as the founder of their church. But whether it was St Mark or another who brought the Faith to Alexandria, Christianity was early introduced into Egypt, as we should expect it to be. Farther along the coast, Carthage, too, early became an important Christian centre. Something like a hundred Christian churches had been founded by the end of the first century, about a quarter of them in the West.

How did the Faith first reach our own shores? And when? Certainly it was long before the Romans left, and almost certainly it was brought in, in the first place, by Christian traders. We must not forget Christian soldiers, but at first few if any soldiers seem to have been Christians.

2

A Christian Convert

Within the limits of the Acts of the Apostles—about thirty
years—we see one tremendous change: the Gospel, rejected by
the Jews, finds acceptance by the Gentiles. If you were a convert
in those days you would probably be a Gentile. Remembering
that Christians were not being persecuted everywhere or all the
time, we shall try to stand in the shoes of such a convert during
days when there was no persecution.

After A.D. 64, however, which is the date of Nero's—the
first large—persecution, Christians were never safe from attack.
There was little point, therefore, in becoming a convert unless
you were very much in earnest. Public opinion would certainly
be against you, because the Christian did not fit into the pattern
of life in the ancient world. If he had, he would never have been
accused of turning the world upside down. Becoming a Christian
might mean changing your job; it would in any event mark you
off and cut you off from your neighbours. For example, you
could no longer observe the festivals and customs which they
observed, whether they believed in the old gods and goddesses or
not. Many did not believe in them and many did not believe in
a life after death—they were those who "having no hope and
without God in the world" (Eph. 2. 12), lived only for the
moment; which did not usually then, and does not usually now,
mean a life of high principles. Morals were lax and vice flourished. It was a cruel and grey world.

AN INQUIRER
Most likely then it was because you were thoroughly unhappy
about all this that you first took notice of Christianity. You
could have come into touch with it in various ways—perhaps
by listening to a preacher in the public square (cf. Acts 17. 17);
or by going to a talk in a hall or lecture-room (cf. Acts 19. 9, 10).
In the quite early days you might already have been a "god-
fearer", i.e. one who had become attached to the Jewish syna-

10

gogue and tried to keep the Jewish moral law but without becoming an actual proselyte or convert to Judaism. In that case you might have heard the Gospel proclaimed in the synagogue, perhaps by St Paul himself. The Apostle's practice was, as we know, to proclaim Christ first in the synagogue.

A few years later, in the second century, you might have got hold of one of the writings of the Christian Apologists, men who wrote to explain the Faith to Jews and pagans and to defend it against attack. This is what one of them, the author of the *Epistle to Diognetus*, wrote about A.D. 140: "They (the Christians) exist in the flesh, but they live not after the flesh. They spend their existence upon earth, but their citizenship is in heaven. They obey the established laws, but in their lives they surpass the laws. They love all men, and are persecuted by all. . . . They do good, and are punished as evil-doers." But such writings would not have impressed you if ordinary Christians had not borne out what was claimed for them. If you were one who was dissatisfied with all that paganism could offer, it might have become clear to you that the Christians possessed what you were seeking. "Something happened to the men who associated with Jesus,"[1] and this was true of others besides those who had known Him in the days of His flesh. In Christ new light had broken into the world, and this life Christians possessed. That was why their lives were not as other men's. When you got a Christian friend to introduce you to a local congregation, what decided you would almost certainly be what you knew of ordinary Christian folk—it may be, when you met them at your work. Justin Martyr (A.D. 163) says that it was not uncommon for people to be converted because of the impression made by the honesty of Christians in their business dealings. We can understand why most Christians will have been converted one by one or in little groups.

Your next step would be to ask for baptism. At first, once you could say that Jesus is Lord, this was conferred quickly. The confession of faith attributed in the Authorized Version to the Ethiopian eunuch, "I believe that Jesus Christ is the Son of God",[2] reflects primitive practice (Acts 8. 37; and see also 16.

[1] K. Latourette: *History of the Expansion of Christianity*, vol. 1, p. 167; and cf. Acts 4. 13.
[2] These words are omitted in the oldest Bible MSS., which is why R.V. does not include them. But if someone wrote them on the margin of his copy of Acts, and so they found their way into the text, it must have been quite early, for they reflect the early baptismal custom.

30–33). Usually, following upon the water-baptism, would come the laying on of hands (cf. Acts 19. 1–7); thereafter you would be regarded as a member of the great Church and of the local congregation, which was the Body of Christ in that place. Every Lord's Day (the name is found in Rev. 1. 10), which was the day of the resurrection, you and all the other members would meet for "the breaking of the bread" and to share the "cup of blessing", i.e. for Holy Communion. An early name was the Eucharist (thanksgiving) and from the first this was the Church's chief act of worship.

INSTRUCTION

St Paul taught "from house to house" (Acts 20. 20). You too would be taught what your baptism meant and, now you were a Christian, what you ought to do. You would be taught much of this by heart, repeating it over and over again. In this way, also, you would learn some of our Lord's sayings, and stories about Him such as we find in the Gospels. Both in the Jewish and Gentile worlds learning by heart was the common method of instruction.

You would be taught what to "put on" and what to "put off". To "put off" lying, guile, hypocrisy, blasphemy, envy, wrath, malice; to "put off" all filth, and lust, and uncleanness. Not to steal. But to "put on" compassion, kindness, humility. Humility meant obedience to those who were over you, but it also meant charity (love) in all your dealings with others. You would be taught to be forbearing and forgiving. To work honestly for your living, to be truthful, to live purely, to walk no longer in darkness but as children of the light. So walking— in the Spirit—you *would* be well-pleasing to God; and what better encouragement could you have than the knowledge that you had "put on Christ" (Gal. 3. 27) and been sealed with the Holy Spirit (Eph. 1. 13; 4. 30; 2 Cor. 1. 21, 22), marked as God's for all eternity? You would be taught to worship, to offer "spiritual sacrifices, acceptable to God" (1 Pet. 2. 5); to watch and pray, to stand fast if tempted, to resist the Devil. All this was the common Christian teaching; you would have been taught it by any Christian teacher anywhere. (Cf. for example, Col. 3. 8–14; Jas. 4. 7–8, 10; 1 Pet. 2. 1, and 5. 5–9.)

THE HIPPOLYTAN RITE OF CHRISTIAN INITIATION

After a time baptism was not given so quickly. There would be more teaching first. Hippolytus of Rome, in his *Apostolic*

Tradition, written about A.D. 215, has told us how new members were admitted in his day. First, you would be questioned as to why you wanted to be a Christian and as to the work you did; then, if approved, you would enter on a long period of probation, Hippolytus says three years, but it was sometimes not quite so long. All this time, while you were a catechumen (one under instruction for baptism), you were not allowed to pray with the faithful at the actual offering of the Eucharist, but were sent out after the Scripture readings and the sermon. Even small places in those days had their own bishop and the bishop would dismiss you and the other catechumens after the prayers which followed the sermon, with your own special blessing. (Hippolytus does not say this but we know that this was the practice and that the bishop raised his hand in blessing.) So naturally you would long for the day when you need not go out but could "join in prayer with all the people" (Hippolytus).

Before it came you would have to undergo a most searching examination of your life, and then attend preparation classes every day for perhaps a month or six weeks. This would be just before Easter, for Easter was the great baptismal season. In those days Christians used to keep an all-night vigil during the night of Holy Saturday, and you would join in this vigil. Then at cockcrow the great moment came. First, the bishop would bless the water in the baptismal tank (running water, if it could be arranged). Then a priest (called in those days a presbyter, of which priest is a short form) would tell you to make your renunciation. You said: "I renounce thee, Satan, and all thy servants and all thy works." You then entered the water, a deacon going in with you. The priest, standing at the side, asked: "Dost thou believe in God, the Father Almighty?" You replied, "I believe", and thereupon you would be plunged, probably by the deacon, under the water. Next, the priest asked you, "Dost thou believe in Christ Jesus, the Son of God, who was born of the Holy Ghost and the Virgin Mary?" and so on, repeating the middle section of the Creed, in much the same words that we use now. You said, "I believe", and a second time you were plunged under the water. Then the priest said: "Dost thou believe in the Holy Ghost and the holy Church and the resurrection of the flesh?" Again you replied, "I believe", and for the third and last time you were submerged.

After leaving the water you would dress and go into church for your confirmation. The bishop would lay his hand upon you and pray that God who had made you worthy to obtain forgiveness of sins would fill you with the Holy Spirit of grace that you might serve Him according to His will. Then he would anoint you on the forehead with consecrated oil (chrism), signing you with the cross. The bishop said: "I anoint thee with holy oil in the Lord, the Father Almighty and Christ Jesus and the Holy Ghost," and, as he signed you, "The Lord be with thee", to which you replied, "And with thy spirit". And immediately, says Hippolytus, you were to "join in prayer with all the people". It would now be dawn and the Holy Communion would begin at once. The deacons would bring the bread and wine to the bishop. He would begin, "The Lord be with you." "And with thy spirit." "Lift up your hearts." "We lift them up unto the Lord." "Let us give thanks to the Lord." "It is meet and right." The Church has gone on saying this dialogue of the Preface from Hippolytus's day, and probably from some time before that, till now. The bishop would say the Eucharistic prayer, and then, for the first time, you would make your communion. Besides receiving the bread and wine, you and the others making a first communion, would also be given a cup containing water and a cup of milk mixed with honey. You received these before you received the wine. This seems most confusing to us, and the custom soon died out, but the purpose of the water, it seems, was to extend the baptismal washing to the inner man; and the cup of milk and honey symbolized your entry into the Promised Land.

Having waited so long to "join in prayer with all the people", do you think that you would want to break the custom of those early days of *all* the faithful meeting for their communion *every* Sunday?[1]

[1] The quotations from Hippolytus's *The Apostolic Tradition* are taken from the translation, with introduction and notes, by B. S. Easton.

14

3

Worship and Ministry

HOW CHRISTIANS WORSHIPPED

For three centuries the Christians of Rome buried their dead in the catacombs, those underground galleries in the hills just outside the walls of Aurelian. They were buried one above the other in sepulchres cut out of the rock and sealed with a slab of marble or with tiles. There were five such burial places. But they were not used only for burials. In many places the rock was cut away in such a manner as to leave a flat, table-like slab on which the Eucharist could be celebrated in the presence of at least some worshippers. Or we find a deep basin, with steps leading down to it: we can guess the use of that. The Christians worshipped in catacombs (there were also catacombs at Naples) because they were reasonably safe there. There was no secret about their meeting in them, but Romans respected the dead and hesitated to interfere with a burial-place. Only in the last two persecutions—under Valerian and Diocletian—were Christian cemeteries confiscated.

But it would be quite wrong if we got the idea that Christian worship was always hidden away in some underground place, in depressing, and perhaps rather squalid surroundings. That was not so. The catacombs were dark, and though there were a few shafts which let in a little daylight and air, you needed a lamp, but they were never depressing or squalid—the paintings and inscriptions on the walls and ceilings show that. We find fruit and flowers, animals and birds, and symbolic drawings such as the dove (representing the Holy Spirit), the ship, the anchor, the shepherd (a beardless boy, for the figure was symbolical, not a life-like portrait of Christ). Even the face of Christ found on one of the ceilings can hardly have been a true likeness, although it shows Christ bearded and much as He is usually depicted to-day. The inscriptions strike a note of joy. Contrast the pagan epitaph, commonly used of slaves, "I was not, I was. I am not, I care not," with the kind of inscription found in the catacombs: "Live in peace", "Victorious in Christ", or, on the tomb of a child, "Pray for thy parents".

15

Mostly, however, Christians did not meet in catacombs. They worshipped in private houses, and the setting here might as easily be splendid as plain. One thing is certain, it would not be squalid. The oldest known church-building to be preserved, that found in the ruins of Dura, in Mesopotamia, once an important town on the high-road to the East, had been constructed out of a private house. The building dates from about A.D. 230 and has now been re-erected in a museum at Yale; a picture appears

from "*The Church of our Fathers*" (by permission)

THE OLDEST KNOWN CHURCH BUILDING

in Roland Bainton's *The Church of our Fathers* and is reproduced here. The church had a proper baptistry although it had once been a house. The picture shows the baptistry with a painting on the wall behind of the Good Shepherd with his sheep and, on the left, one of Adam and Eve standing by a tree. A beginning had been made at decorating the main room similarly with pictures from the Old and New Testaments, when the church was destroyed. From Cirta (now Constantine, in Algeria) a list of church property made when the building was seized in A.D. 303 shows that the church possessed, among other things, many baptismal tunics for men and women, two

16

chalices of gold and six of silver, six silver dishes, silver lamps, bronze lamps and bronze candlesticks.[1]

THE LORD'S OWN SERVICE

Yet the service would be simple. The bishop would have his seat (throne) on the far side of the table, in the centre, at the end of the room. On either side of him would be the priests (presbyters). There would be several of them and several deacons, some of whom would keep the door, for none but the faithful might be present. But the clergy would not be differently dressed from the laity. Sunday by Sunday, very early in the morning before the day's work began (for Sunday was a working day in the Roman Empire up to A.D. 321), little bands of men and women, with a few children, met to do as Christ had commanded, to break the bread and drink of the cup. These were the faithful. After the bishop had said: "Peace be with you", each would place on a dish on the table a few pieces of bread and pour into a cup a little wine from a bottle which he had brought, and the children would add a little water. Some of the bread and wine would then be set aside for distribution to the poor, the rest offered at the communion. At the communion the bread of the Sacrament would be received from the bishop, the cup would be proffered by a deacon. You came to the table for your communion and communicated standing.[2] Afterwards you would be given some of the consecrated bread to take home in a silver box which you carried, so that you might make your communion at home during the week. You might have met Sunday by Sunday in some places for a good many years quite unmolested. On the other hand you might never have gone home after the service at all. Somebody might have lodged a complaint, and you and the others would have found yourselves arrested and at once put on trial. What that might have meant we shall see in the next chapter.

THE CHRISTIAN MINISTRY

But before we do this we must attempt to trace the origins of the Christian ministry and see how it developed. This is very important because divergent views about the ministry are the principal barrier to the "growing together", and ultimate reunion of the Anglican and Nonconformist churches. It is

[1] For the list see Gregory Dix: *The Shape of the Liturgy*, p. 24. The next paragraph is taken largely from Dix.
[2] See the interesting picture in *The Church of our Fathers*, p. 35.

also very difficult. We depend for our knowledge on a few passages in the New Testament which tell us something, but not all, that we should like to know. Different inferences can be, and are, drawn from them. We depend also on what we see the Church doing in the generations following the age of the Apostles, and here there are gaps. Dom Gregory Dix says that it would be generally agreed to-day that by about A.D. 160, or not much after, "the historic 'threefold ministry' of bishop, presbyters, and deacons is in ascertained possession of the whole field of Church Order in the Great Church".[1] Can we see how this came about?

THE TWELVE

First of all we will go to the New Testament. Our Lord left no clear-cut directions about the ministry, but one thing He undoubtedly did—He instituted the Twelve. Jesus "appointed (A.V. 'ordained', the Greek word is 'made') twelve, that they might be with him, and that he might send them forth to preach" (Mk. 3. 14). The Greek verb used here for "send forth" is the verb corresponding to the noun *apostolos*, "apostle". When the Twelve returned from the mission on which our Lord sent them "by two and two", Mark calls them "apostles" (6. 30, and cf. Lk. 6. 13), but the usual name during Christ's lifetime seems to have been the Twelve.

An apostle is someone sent with a message or as an agent, someone bearing the authority of the person or body sending him and empowered to act on their behalf. There was a similar noun in Hebrew, *shaliach*, with its corresponding verb, and the Rabbis had a saying "the 'sent' of a man is as himself". We might compare Matt. 10. 40 (part of our Lord's address to the Twelve after their institution): "He that receiveth you receiveth me, and he that receiveth me receiveth him that sent me." After His resurrection, on the evening of Easter Day Christ renewed His commission: "As my Father hath sent me, even so send I you. . . . Receive ye the Holy Ghost (literally, 'Take Holy Spirit') . . ." (See Jn. 20. 21–23.) We should notice that none of the Gospels says how our Lord appointed or "made" the Twelve in the first instance; when He renewed His commission after the resurrection He "breathed on them". When St Matthias took the place of the traitor Judas and "was numbered with the eleven apostles" (Acts 1. 26), we are not told

[1] *The Apostolic Ministry*, p. 190.

that the Eleven laid their hands on him. He was chosen by lot after prayer, the appointment being regarded as coming direct from our Lord Himself. St Paul similarly regarded his apostleship as conferred direct by the risen Lord. He was not ordained by the other Apostles. We have seen that others besides the Twelve were called Apostles; we might add also St James the Lord's brother (Gal. 1, 19), who became the head of the church at Jerusalem.

APOSTLES AND ELDERS, BISHOPS AND DEACONS

We must examine some other passages.

(i) Acts 6. 1–6. Here the Apostles give up some of their ministerial work to others. But what were the Seven? They are not called deacons and the New Testament does not mention deacons in the church at Jerusalem. It does mention elders (Acts 11. 30; 15. 22; 21. 17–18), and some scholars think the Seven were in fact elders. Anyway, they were ordained to a subordinate ministry.

What makes the passage so important is that it tells us exactly how the appointment was made. The initiative came from the Apostles but the people selected the men and presented them to the Apostles, who appointed them by prayer with the laying on of hands. The act was in no sense the private act of the Apostles, it was that of the whole Christian community, but the part the Apostles took was essential to it. We must suppose they acted as they did in view of our Lord's commission. The method they adopted was modelled on the practice of contemporary Judaism. Rabbis were ordained in this way, and so were the members of a local Jewish presbytery or council of elders, where the other members each laid their hands on the head of a newly elected member. We may say, in fact, that Christian ordination "is simply a Jewish rite *plus the difference Christ makes*", which of course is all the difference.[1] May we not believe that the Apostles acted as they did under the guidance of the Holy Spirit; that what they did was according to the mind of Christ?

We should notice the word "elder". The Greek word is *presbuteros*, "presbyter", of which "priest" is, as we have seen, a shortened form. Originally it meant an older person and it is found in that sense in the New Testament. Most members of councils would in the early days be older persons, but the term

---

[1] Cf. W. K. Lowther Clarke in *Episcopacy Ancient and Modern*, ed. C. Jenkins and K. D. Mackenzie, p. 42.

came to apply to office rather than age. We can think of the elders at Jerusalem administering the Church there under James the Lord's brother; they may or may not have conducted its worship. Later on this was to be a principal function of the priesthood; to begin with, the function of the presbyters seems to have been more like that of a church council.

(ii) Phil. 1. 1; 2 Tim. 1. 6; 1 Tim. 4. 14. We come now to the Pauline Churches. St Paul's usual practice was to appoint a regular ministry in the Churches which he founded. The local council of elders would then be responsible for teaching, discipline and the conduct of worship, but always under the Apostle who kept the supreme control in his own hands. Why does he greet the bishops and deacons at Philippi and make no mention of the elders? Almost certainly because bishops and elders were one and the same: we may speak of them as presbyter-bishops. This is the obvious inference from Acts 20. 17, 28, where St Paul sends for the Ephesian elders and then addresses them as bishops, that is, overseers. Notice too that although St Paul ordains Timothy, the elders ("the presbytery") are associated with him, probably by placing their hands over his. St Paul, it seems clear, kept the right to appoint to the ministry in his own hands or in those of "apostolic men" like St Timothy or St Titus acting as his delegates.

(iii) Tit. 1. 5, 7. Titus in this passage is charged "to appoint elders (presbyters) in every city" of Crete, then "the bishop" is mentioned in the singular. Too much should not be made of this perhaps; nevertheless someone possessing gifts of leadership and energy had to preside over the local "presbytery" or governing body. He alone would come to be called *episcopos*, overseer, bishop, and the rest were simply presbyters. Not much after A.D. 100 churches like those of Antioch and Corinth had a single bishop, and in the second century the single bishop, with presbyters and deacons under him, became the rule. Unlike the first century apostle, who, except in the case of St James the Lord's brother at Jerusalem, did not stay in one locality, the second century bishop did, but otherwise his functions, which included the right to ordain, were much the same. The identity appeared to Dr Kirk too close to be a pure coincidence; he regarded the duties of the Apostles as having been handed on deliberately with the consent of the Church.[1] This, it need hardly be said, is the kind of inference which one will draw and another will not.

[1] See *The Apostolic Ministry*, p. 10.

THE PRINCIPLE OF SUCCESSION

The opinion expressed by Dr Kirk gains a certain amount of support from what is usually called the *First Epistle of Clement*, a letter written by Clement in the name of the Roman Church and sent to the Church at Corinth. The letter witnesses to a principle of succession: "Jesus Christ was sent out from God. Christ then is from God, and the Apostles from Christ. Both therefore issued from the will of God with due order." The bishops (that is, probably, the presbyter-bishops, for the letter which mentions both presbyters and bishops seems, like Acts 20, to regard them as belonging to the same ministerial grade) and deacons were appointed by the Apostles, who "ordained that at their death their ministry should pass into the hands of other tried men". But this does not really tell us very much beyond confirming—and this is important—the principle of ministerial succession. How the change from apostle to bishop, or from presbyter-bishop to bishop as distinct from and superior to presbyter was made, we do not know. We may believe that the need of the Church necessitated the step and that the Church was divinely guided in making it.

Historically it can neither be proved nor disproved that the grace of orders has been handed on through ordainer to ordained, the ordainer always being an apostle or a bishop or (at the beginning) a presbyter-bishop, and there being no break in the chain linking the episcopate of to-day with the first bishops whom the Apostles themselves appointed. So far as concerns the Church of England, there was no break at the Reformation; if there be a break, its place is in the earliest age, before the threefold ministry became everywhere established. But this has to be remembered. Wherever we see the Church actually perpetuating its ministry, it is always, right up to the Reformation, through the laying on of apostolic or at least episcopal hands—it being recognized, of course, that although the power to transmit the gift was the bishop's, in virtue of his consecration, the ministerial gift itself came from God. The universal belief of later ages was that the Church was directly descended from the Apostles.

This has been called somewhat disparagingly a "pipe-line" view of the ministry; but the phrase "the Apostolic Succession" means, or should mean, more than mere succession, and the principle of ministerial succession by ordination should furnish a guarantee which reinforces that provided by a succession of

bishops in any particular see that the faith which is taught is
the Apostolic faith. The reason why, in the early days, Churches
which could claim an Apostle as founder proudly produced
their lists of bishops linking their own day with that of the
Apostles in an unbroken sequence, was that this seemed to
them to guarantee the faith which was held, and which it was
their duty to preserve and pass on intact.

THE NON-EPISCOPAL CHURCHES AND THE MINISTRY

The Reformation nowhere began with an attack on the ministry, but at the Reformation new theories arose, and with many
tradition was at a discount. All Nonconformists—and some
Anglicans—would maintain that it does not matter whether
the claim to Apostolic descent on the part of the ministry is true
or not; and that, even if the threefold ministry may have been
best once, it does not follow that God intended it to be the
pattern of the Church's ministry for ever. Those Anglicans
who agree would still, presumably, say that government by
bishops is the best form of Church order, but Nonconformists,
on practical as well as theoretical grounds, are not easily con-
vinced of this.

Fundamentally the non-episcopalian bases his views of the
ministry on our Lord's saying: "Where two or three are gathered together in my name, there am I in the midst of them"
(Matt. 18. 20). As Dr T. W. Manson puts it: "There is one essential ministry"—not, as the writers in *The Apostolic Ministry*
argued, the episcopate—but "the perpetual ministry of the
Risen Lord, present . . . where His people are gathered in His
name, and renewing to each generation the gifts they need to
continue *His* ministry."[1] Christ, present in each congregation
or community, empowers and enables it to perpetuate the
ministry in any way it chooses, by a laying on of hands or otherwise. Most of the divided communions of present-day Christendom, apart from the great stream represented by the Roman
and the Orthodox Churches, are non-episcopal, and they make
a really telling point when they instance their undeniable
achievements. God has blessed their ministries: of that there
can be no doubt. But the Anglican need not deny this, nor need
he deny that the Lord's Supper, though not administered by a
priest, conveys spiritual benefits to those who partake of it in

[1] *The Church's Ministry*, p. 76. This short book is to be recommended
to the Anglican who would understand the Nonconformist point of view.

faith. To doubt this is to doubt the love of God. Yet, when all is said, the Anglican may feel that, however attractive the non-episcopal theory is in its simplicity, it was nowhere heard of until about four hundred years ago. Against this he will set the solid tradition of the earlier centuries.

4

Persecution

THE CHARGES AGAINST CHRISTIANS

If you had been a Christian in the early days you might, in some places, have gone on worshipping for years and not have met with trouble. On the other hand you might have gone out some Sunday morning, very early, to join in worship with the rest of the Christians where you lived, and never have come home. Suppose someone had lodged a complaint against you, you would probably have found yourself charged with taking part in an unlawful assembly. Judaism in the Roman Empire had a legally recognized right to exist. Christianity had no such right. Rome was afraid of secret organizations; it scented treason in an unauthorized gathering. How great indeed was the fear of societies is seen in Trajan's prohibition of a fire-brigade. Religion, moreover, was looked upon not as a matter of conviction but as the affair of a state department. Except in the case of the Jews, religious activities had to be organized in a way which provided for the worship of the reigning Emperor. That was how you proved your loyalty.

Orders issued by the Emperor Domitian describe him as "our Lord and God", and you were expected to address him as such in speech and writing. Trajan was "God, the invincible son of God", and Nero had an altar erected to him in his lifetime inscribed "To Nero God the deliverer for ever". How could Christians countenance that sort of thing? Pagans probably thought it nonsense, but to Christians it was blasphemy. There was one loop-hole: you could sometimes get a measure of protection by registering as a burial-club (there were registered clubs of every possible kind), but a religious organization proper had to make provision for the worship of Rome and the Emperor. They spoke of *Dea Roma*, making the spirit of Rome into a goddess. Magistrates, so it appears, had considerable power of discretion and they certainly often shut their eyes— for most Romans were by nature tolerant; but if someone brought a complaint, they had to take notice and they seem to

24

have acted on the principle that if a defendant pleaded guilty he could not be acquitted.[1] If Christians refused to swear by the genius of the Emperor or to throw a few grains of incense on a fire burning in a tripod-bowl before the Emperor's statue, and so to show themselves loyal subjects, then they must pay the penalty. So long as the State regarded Christians as a Jewish sect they were safe, for Jews were allowed to practise their faith without adding Emperor-worship; but Christians ceased to be so regarded at the time of Nero. Indeed, the jealousy of the Jews became a contributory cause of Christian persecution.

And the penalty? Imprisonment; perhaps being sent to the lead-mines of Sardinia (you did not usually live long there); or perhaps being thrown to the beasts. For centuries the Roman mob had had "free shows" provided for them by consuls and Emperors—chariot-races, with their breath-taking turns at full speed and their rivalry between the Whites, the Greens, the Blues, the Reds; and their wild-beast shows, when lions, tigers, panthers, even elephants, were slaughtered to make a Roman holiday. When the mob "grew bored with watching armed huntsmen pitted against beasts of prey, fights to the death were staged between the beasts themselves." Then Augustus—who was Emperor when Christ was born—"started a new fashion, by causing a notorious bandit to be dropped into a cage of wild beasts. The idea caught on, and the throwing of unarmed men *ad bestias* became a common verdict in the Courts and a popular spectacle in the amphitheatre. Christians were the victims most frequently demanded . . . and he who stands to-day in the gaunt ruins of the Colosseum can imagine, if he will, what it felt like to stand there in Nero's day, while the Emperor stared down on the amphitheatre through his emerald eye-glass, and there rose from the crowded tiers a mighty roar as 50,000 people yelled in unison, 'Christianos ad leonem!'"[2]

NERO

Nero had reigned ten years before he staged the first great persecution, and this, though fiendishly cruel, was confined to Rome. It had nothing to do with Christians not conforming to the State religion—it was Domitian, twenty years later, who insisted on Emperor-worship. Nero charged the Christians with the specific crime of arson, with having started the fire of Rome

[1] Cf. E. T. Merrill: *Essays in Early Christian History*, p. 71.
[2] H. Grose-Hodge: *Roman Panorama*, pp. 223–5.

which raged for nine days in the summer of A.D. 64, and destroyed more than half the city. There were grave suspicions that he started the fire himself. "Consequently," says the Roman historian Tacitus, "to get rid of the report, Nero fastened the guilt and inflicted the most exquisite tortures on a class hated for their abominations, called Christians by the populace. . . . Accordingly, an arrest was first made of all who pleaded guilty; then, upon their information, an immense multitude was convicted, not so much of the crime of firing the city, as of hatred against mankind. Mockery of every sort was added to their deaths. Covered with the skins of beasts, they were torn by dogs and perished, or were nailed to crosses, or were doomed to the flames and burnt, to serve as a nightly illumination when daylight had expired. Nero offered his gardens for the spectacle, and was exhibiting a show in the circus, while he mingled with the people in the dress of a charioteer or stood aloft on a car. Hence, even for criminals who deserve extreme and exemplary punishment, there arose a feeling of compassion; for it was not, as it seemed, for the public good, but to glut one man's cruelty that they were being destroyed."[1]

Tacitus was a boy of about ten when this happened and may even have seen it. We do not know the number put to death. Historians think that Tacitus's "immense multitude" may not mean more than "many". He tried to be fair but he had no love for any Emperor—he would have liked the old Republic back —and he clearly did not understand the Christians. Nero's persecution, however, stands by itself. It began a few months after the fire; but persecution continued for the four years that were left of his reign.

THE SCILLITAN MARTYRS

On July 17th in A.D. 180, seven men and five women, from Scillium in Numidia, were sentenced to death at Carthage. Here we see the more ordinary, day to day hazards which Christians ran, and we see the Roman magistrate in a very favourable light. He sat with a body of advisers, but it was he who conducted the case and passed sentence. In this instance the proconsul clearly did not want to condemn the accused persons. Again and again he tried to get them to swear by the genius of the Emperor. He gave them every chance.

"Saturninus the proconsul said: Be not partakers of this folly.

[1] B. J. Kidd: *Documents*, vol. 1, No. 22.

Cittinus said: We have none other to fear, save only our Lord God, who is in heaven.

Donata said: Honour to Caesar as Caesar; but fear to God.

Vestia said: I am a Christian.

Secunda said: What I am, that I wish to be.

Saturninus the proconsul said to Speratus: Dost thou persist in being a Christian?

Speratus said: I am a Christian. And with him they all agreed.

Saturninus the proconsul said: Will ye have a space to consider?

Speratus said: In a matter so straightforward there is no considering. . . .

Saturninus the proconsul said: Have a delay of thirty days and bethink yourselves.

Speratus said a second time: I am a Christian. And with him they all agree." [1] So the order for their execution was made.

MOB VIOLENCE

Where we see Christians charged with the most monstrous crimes—abominable immorality, cannibalism, sometimes atheism (because they would not worship the old gods)—mob fury was usually responsible. So we find the aged Polycarp, Bishop of Smyrna, accused of atheism (A.D. 156). His reply, on being asked to revile Christ, is famous: "Eighty and six years have I served Him, and He hath done me no wrong: how then can I blaspheme my King who saved me?" Probably in those days not many children were admitted to membership of the Church when they were very small, though there is provision for their baptism in the rite of Hippolytus, others speaking for them; but it looks as though Polycarp had been. Now as an old man he won the martyr's crown. He was burnt at the stake to please the rabble. But it is easy to see how some of the charges brought against the Christians originated from the secrecy with which they surrounded their rites. They worshipped behind closed doors, and people will always imagine the worst. They had heard something about eating someone's body and drinking someone's blood; so they said Christians sacrificed new-born babes and feasted on them. However, long before persecution ceased, even pagans knew better than that. Persons who, when persecuted, show no hatred to those who oppress them, are not that kind of people.

[1] Kidd: *Documents*, vol. 1, No. 67.

THE GREAT PERSECUTORS

We shall not attempt to describe the various persecutions. Let it suffice to make a short list of those Emperors whose names have come down as the great persecutors, though it must not be imagined for one moment that Christians only suffered under them.

Nero: from A.D. 64 to his death in 68.

Domitian: A.D. 81–96. There had been Christians in "Caesar's household" (Phil. 4. 22) from an early date. Domitian struck at the highest, not only at Christians, because he feared conspiracy. He promoted Emperor-worship and, as Lightfoot said, struck down "one here and one there . . . harassing the Church with an agony of suspense."

Decius: A.D. 249–51. This was the most severe general persecution up to that time; Rome, Gaul, Spain, Africa, Egypt, Palestine, Greece and Asia Minor were all affected.

Valerian: A.D. 257–8. Again persecution was severe and widespread. St Cyprian, Bishop of Carthage, and a great Christian teacher, was beheaded.

Diocletian: from A.D. 303–313. Although he abdicated on May 1st, 305, the persecution is always known by his name. It was more severe in the East than the West; at its very outset the George who is probably England's patron saint was burnt at Nicomedia for high treason —he had torn down notices ordering the destruction of churches and of the Scriptures. There were, however, martyrdoms at Rome, and in Britain (so Bede tells us) St Alban suffered.

Diocletian, who was an able organizer, should be remembered not simply as a persecutor but because he divided the Roman Empire into two. He made Maximian, a soldier, Augustus or Emperor in the West, with his capital at Milan, while he himself remained Augustus in the East, where Nicomedia, which was just in Asia, was the capital city. Each Augustus had a second-in-command, called a Caesar, and the plan was that the Caesar should automatically succeed the Augustus as Emperor on the latter's death or after twenty years. The two Caesars had their headquarters at strategically important places on the Rhine and the Danube, Trier (Trèves) and Sirmium, which thus became also important administrative centres. So we get the following set-up, with the names of the first Augusti (Emperors) and the first Caesars given after the name of their headquarters.

WEST	EAST
Milan—Maximian	Nicomedia—Diocletian
Trier—Constantius	Sirmium—Galerius.

For nineteen years all was peaceful. Then Diocletian's second-in-command, Galerius, who was a bitter pagan, pre-

Picture Post Library

THE EMPEROR DIOCLETIAN

vailed on the Emperor to attack Christianity. It is possible that he had discovered a plot, in which Christians were implicated, to divert the succession from himself and on this account pressed Diocletian to persecute. Diocletian's wife, Prisca, and his daughter, Valeria, who were both Christians, were compelled to sacrifice. Then in 305 when Diocletian retired, Galerius became the eastern Augustus—which accounts for the great suffering of the East.

Of course some Christians fell away. Some denied the Faith; some saved themselves by obtaining a certificate which said

29

they had sacrificed when in fact they had not. The problem then rose as to how to deal with them when they wanted to re-enter the Church. Those who had actually sacrificed were generally excluded until they were on their death-bed. But in the main Christians stood fast. "No other of the faiths of mankind, religious or political," says Professor Latourette, "has quite so extensive a record of violent and bitter opposition to its growth"[1]; and yet it not merely won, it turned the world upside down, and that within three hundred years. Should a catechumen be arrested, he was taught not to hesitate to bear his testimony: if he should be killed he would be baptized in his own blood. The blood of the martyrs is the seed of the Church. Yet this is not the whole story. We have to remember that in the third century there were two long periods when Christianity was not persecuted—before the outbreak under Diocletian there was a period of quiet lasting forty years. During these periods the Church progressed rapidly.

[1] *History of the Expansion of Christianity*, i, p. 135.

5

The Peace of the Church

Since it was Galerius who really instigated Diocletian's persecution, Diocletian's abdication on May 1st, 305, did not make
life easier for Christians in the East. In the West there was little
persecution. Constantius, if he allowed some churches to be
destroyed, protected the persons of Christians. He was a
humane, kindly man, and, although not a Christian, a believer
in one supreme God.

THE SON OF CONSTANTIUS

Diocletian, when he retired, forced Maximian to abdicate as
well, in accordance with the original plan. The two Caesars
now automatically became Emperors. Constantius, the new
Emperor of the West, succeeded to the Empire when he was in
Britain. He had arrived in Britain in 296, four years after his
appointment as Caesar, and had lived there almost continu-
ously, making York his capital. He had come in the first place to
quell a revolt, and stayed on to restore the Roman government.
He seems to have liked the island and did not want to return
to Trier. He even returned to York from Rome after becoming Emperor of the West, and it was at York that he died
in 306.

His son Constantine, when his father died, was with Galerius
in the East. He was passed over for the succession and kept a
prisoner. But he got away and rode post-haste across Europe,
reaching York, where his father's legions hailed him as Emperor.
For as long as five or six years he remained in Britain, while as
many as six Emperors, including himself, parcelled out the
Empire and quarrelled and fought for the mastery. And all the
while the persecution of Christians in the East continued
steadily. Then we find the six Emperors reduced to two. In
September 312, Constantine crossed the Alps; in late October,
at the Milvian Bridge close to Rome, he defeated and routed
the army of Maxentius, Maximian's son, who was himself
drowned.

31

HOC VINCE

This battle, by the Tiber, is one of the decisive battles of the world. It decided Constantine to become a Christian and that decision meant the peace of the Church. The odds seemed so heavily against him; Maxentius commanded four times as large an army as he. But before the battle Constantine and, so we are told, his soldiers too, saw something which they believed to be a vision—a cross of light in the noonday sky, with the inscription *Hoc Vince*, "In this conquer". Was it a miracle? Our Lord said we were not to look for signs; but Constantine undoubtedly saw something in which he read a message to himself and, going forward, conquered. Yet we need to remember that even if it was this victory which finally decided him to become a Christian, he would never have made the decision if he had not first been impressed by the Christians. As Dr Bright has said, "He knew a great thing when he saw it."

THE EDICT OF MILAN

After the battle Constantine went northward to Milan, and there he and Licinius, now the Eastern ruler, who married Constantine's sister, issued in March 313 the famous Edict of Milan, which was a declaration of toleration. This did not mean that Christianity was as yet established as the religion of the Empire, but it did mean that persecution was at an end and that Christians and pagans alike were granted "the free and open exercise" of their faiths. It is a turning-point in Christian history. Except in the East persecution was over; and in the East it was to be over ten years later, when Constantine became sole Emperor. For, in spite of the edict, and a similar proclamation for the East issued by Licinius at Nicomedia, just as Constantine more and more favoured Christianity, so Licinius more and more championed heathenism and set on foot secretly further persecution in the years just before his defeat and death in 323. Once forty Christian soldiers were put to death. The accession of Constantine as sole ruler changed all this, and soon the Christian Church was to become, within the Roman Empire, that very dangerous thing, "the State's darling".

THE COUNCIL OF ARLES

There is, however, one event which we ought to notice in the years before Constantine became sole Emperor. This is the

"Picture Post"

CONSTANTINE THE GREAT (A.D. 288–337).   (See page 31)

("Picture Post" Library)

FROM THE COVERDALE BIBLE.   (See Vol. I, pages 173–4, and Vol. II, pages 191–2)

Paul Popper, Ltd.

THE CHURCH OF ST. SOPHIA TODAY, WITH VIEW OF THE BOSPHORUS IN THE BACKGROUND

At Istanbul, which was formerly Constantinople and was before Byzantium. (See pages 99–109)

calling by him of a council of bishops to meet at Arles, on the Rhône, in southern Gaul, to decide an issue affecting the Church in North Africa. Councils of bishops had met before this, but they had been local gatherings of bishops of one particular district, and for obvious reasons they had been unconnected with the State. But now in 314, the very year following the Edict of Milan, we find Constantine taking the initiative in calling together such a council. Later on, after he had become sole Emperor, we shall find him summoning the first ecumenical or general Council of the Christian Church, which met at Nicaea. But the earlier and smaller Council of Arles has for us this interest, that among the bishops who attended were three from Britain—the Bishop of York, the Bishop of London, and the Bishop of Legionensium. What place is represented by the last name is very uncertain; Lincoln, Caerleon-on-Usk, and Colchester have all been suggested. Evidently, then, there was a properly organized Christian Church in Britain at this time. If the date of the Roman-British church at Silchester, not far from Reading, is between 316 and 325, then possibly one of these bishops consecrated it on his return.

WHAT CONSTANTINE'S CONVERSION MEANT

The Emperor's conversion meant more than the removal of disabilities. It meant that the Church was free at last to develop, and that under State patronage and with an influx of wealthy adherents, it had the means to do so. Churches were built; small churches like the one at Silchester, but great churches also, churches endowed at the public expense and furnished with magnificent copies of the Scriptures, written on vellum, in the form of books not rolls; churches adorned with exquisite mosaics and other treasures of art; churches in which a stately ceremonial became possible and music could develop. This was as it should be, for nowhere is beauty more in place than in the Christian Church. Among the great churches which Constantine built were the original St Peter's on the Vatican in Rome, over the Apostle's tomb, and a church over the tomb of St Paul on the Ostian Way; and at Constantinople the first "Sancta Sophia" or church of the Holy Wisdom, and in the East the Golden Church at Antioch and the great churches at Jerusalem and Bethlehem and on the Mount of Olives. The church of the Holy Sepulchre was to become the holiest sanctuary of Christendom. Even before this some Christians had liked to visit, for the purposes of prayer and of acquiring spiritual merit, the holy places associated with our Lord, but now, with the peace of the Church and the triumph of the Cross, pilgrims began to flock to Jerusalem.

It is true that some of the Fathers thought pilgrimages irrelevant—St Augustine did for one—but their disapproval did nothing to stop the stream of pilgrims, which reached its height in the middle of the fifth century. There were then two hundred monasteries and hospices in and near Jerusalem, and the taking back of relics to the West had become well established. Here we see a danger of a spiritual kind, which the changed status of the Church brought about; but there was ever present the danger of a general lowering of standards, of a compromise with "the world". The very fact that Constantine was unbaptized —he put off baptism and only received it on his death-bed— itself shows a lowering of standards. So does the falling away from the primitive custom of weekly communion. Worldliness and luxury were creeping in.

But now let us notice some further benefits that Constantine's conversion conferred on the Church besides security and material prosperity.

i. Sunday was made a public holiday, except for workers on the land. This was in 321. Christians need no longer get in their worship as best they could before the day's work began and after it ended.

ii. Laws were passed to make life less hard for the poor and for children and (in some things) for slaves. The destitute were to be relieved and foundlings provided for. It was made easier for the slave to become free. Punishments in prison were regulated and branding on the face forbidden. Crucifixion was forbidden.

iii. The prevalent cruelty to animals was checked. Drivers in the public postal service were forbidden to use a heavy stick on their horses. The gladiatorial games were to be stopped—those horrible spectacles where ten thousand beasts might be slain in one day, while "so far from being shocked, the Romans thoroughly enjoyed it". Perhaps, then, it is not surprising that it was three-quarters of a century before the gladiatorial shows were finally put down. Nevertheless these laws of Constantine, with their respect for human life, and their hatred of cruelty, are an indication of the difference which being a Christian made.

CONSTANTINOPLE

In place of Rome Constantine chose a new imperial capital, Byzantium, which he called "New Rome" but which soon came to be known as Constantinople. The solemn inauguration of the city as the new capital took place in 330. The original Byzantium was a small Greek city, a pagan city with its temples, but magnificently situated on the Bosphorus in a fine strategic position at the meeting-point of Europe and Asia, and with a splendid harbour on the Golden Horn. A century later, when in the West the Roman Empire collapsed and barbarian tribes established their rule even in Italy, the Roman Emperor still ruled the rich and populous Eastern provinces from Constantinople. It became a huge city, ten times greater than any city in the West, and "from the end of the fourth century to the middle of the fifteenth, the Byzantine Empire was the centre of a civilization equal to that of any age in brilliancy, certainly the most brilliant known to the Middle Ages, and possibly the only real civilization which prevailed in Europe between the close of the fifth century and the beginning of the eleventh." [1]

Already before Byzantium became Constantine's capital it had one Christian church, St Irene. When Constantine enlarged the city, employing forty thousand Goths to build the new wall, he made it a Christian city; after the solemn inauguration no pagan rites were permitted within its walls. Close by the palace he built the first church of the Holy Wisdom, and close by both was the racecourse, the Circus, which was older than either. It had stood there a hundred years then and it is there to-day. Life in Constantinople centred round these three focal points. For any demonstration, for any public occasion it was to the racecourse that the citizens flocked, as they flocked there also to cheer on the Blues or the Greens in the chariot races. But they flocked to the Cathedral too and the city's bishop or patriarch came to be the next most important person in Constantinople to the Emperor himself.

THE BASILICA

The name basilica—a "royal building"—well describes the type of large church which was built after the Church became the "State's darling"; churches like those built by Constantine which we have already mentioned. But many small churches built about this time follow the same ground plan, if somewhat

---

[1] Prof. C. Diehl, in *Cambridge Mediaeval History*, iv, p. 745.

simplified. Thus St Peter's at Rome had a large atrium or open court, whereas the little Roman-British church at Silchester did not possess one; but in general the plan is the same. There is the semicircular apse at the west end which forms the sanctuary—we should notice that nearly all these churches faced west and not east— and in the nave two rows of pillars separating the central nave from the two aisles. At the east end are three doors and beyond them a colonnaded narthex or covered porch, where the catechumens stood. The altar stood forward to the front of the apse; the bishop (or other celebrant) would stand in the centre behind it, facing down the church. Any ministers assisting would take up their positions on either side of him, also facing down the church.

SILCHESTER

Silchester was already an important town when the Romans came to Britain; it had been the tribal capital of the Atrebates. Roman Silchester was walled, a quarter the size of London, and on the main road between London and the west. Roads leading to York, to Southampton and to Wales also converged on it. But once the traffic on the Roman roads ceased, its decline inevitably followed—it had no water communications. To-day the city of Silchester is farm-land, the site excavated more than half a century ago long since covered up, and some of the monuments have been removed to the museum at Reading.

Roman Silchester had its heathen temples but it also had its Christian church, not nearly so large as the temples, but occupying a prominent position in the heart of the city. (It is fair to say that some uncertainty has been expressed in recent years as to whether the building known as the Roman-British church was a church at all, but the commonly accepted view that it was is followed here.) The walls of the little building, made of rubble (flints in hard mortar), were about two feet thick; the two aisles were probably lower than the central part of the nave. At the east end three doors probably opened into a colonnaded narthex. The two transepts are small, projecting barely two feet beyond the main walls. In the front part of the apse a mosaic, five feet square, marked the spot where the altar—made of wood—would have been placed. It is worn away where presumably the celebrant stood. The altar, which like those in the East would have been almost square, must have covered most of the mosaic. There would have been no seats, but the walls would have been painted and decorated internally. The Romans

36

lighted their buildings adequately by windows, but these were placed high. Probably there were windows in the aisles and in the clerestory (i.e. above the roof of the aisles), and west win-

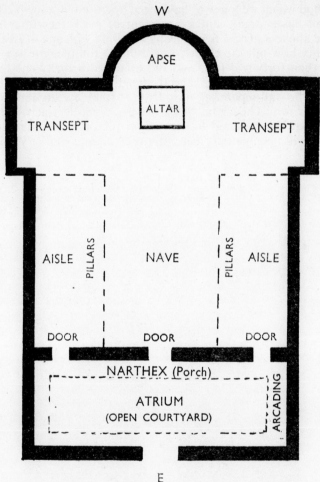

GROUND PLAN OF CHURCH AT SILCHESTER

dows also. They would certainly have had glass in them, probably imported from Gaul where there were glass-works. A great deal of glass has been recovered from Silchester, some of it white bevelled window glass. The shallow pit of brick, eleven feet east of the building, which, it must be remembered, faced west, is too small to have been used for baptisms by immersion, but it might have been used for baptisms by affusion, the candidate standing in the pit while water was poured over his head, a method which we know to have been practised in some places. The pit has a drain, and a pavement of brick tiles four feet square above it. There is no means of telling with any degree of certainty how tall the church was, but the total length was no more than forty-two feet, and the total width thirty-one feet. The apse was six feet deep, and the length of the nave, from the apse to the wall separating nave from narthex, twenty-nine and a quarter feet. The centre of the nave was ten feet across and the two aisles measured five feet from the pillars to the outer wall. It will be apparent, then, that the building was very small indeed.[1]

[1] For the above account I have drawn on *The Book of Silchester*, by James Thompson, F.S.A., 2 vols., 1924. For the church see vol. 2, pp. 401–33.

6

The Flight to the Desert

WORLDLINESS COMES IN

When you have been struggling and struggling against opposition and every sort of difficulty, it may easily throw you out of your stride if, almost overnight, you find yourself having honours of all kinds showered upon you. It was rather like that with the Christian Church. No one expected this sudden change of fortune—that rich and important people would be almost tumbling over one another in their eagerness to become Christians. Only yesterday churches were being destroyed and copies of the Scriptures burned, and the prisons were crowded with bishops, priests, deacons, readers. Not to speak of the martyrdoms. But now people became Christians, or at least joined the Christian Church, who, while a sword hung over every Christian's head, would not for a moment have dreamed of doing so.

Standards were bound to fall. Look on fifty years and see even the clergy—not all of them, but in a big city like Rome enough to be noticeable—becoming worldly, luxury-loving, lazy, vain, avaricious. St Jerome (346–420) said that while devout ladies sold their estates or possessions to give the money in charity, ambitious clergy snapped them up. St Jerome, the greatest Biblical scholar of his age, whose Vulgate translation of the Bible superseded all earlier Latin versions and became the Bible of the Western Church, knew Rome well before retiring to the East in 386, to settle in a monastery at Bethlehem. But we should remember that his strictures applied to a notorious few, men who in the old days would not have been clergy at all, and probably not even Christians. We must not paint too black a picture. Here the evidence of the Emperor Julian, the only Emperor after Constantine who was not a Christian, and who probably reverted to paganism because the Christians who brought him up were such bad ones, is conclusive. He told the pagan priesthood which he tried to revive, to imitate the charity of the Christian clergy and their goodness to the poor, (not confined to poor Christians only). Julian was no persecutor and his short reign (361–3) made no real difference to the religious situation. The character of the Church had not become completely altered. All the same there was a decline, a falling off in quality such as too often takes place when numbers increase rapidly. But still, as from the beginning, there were those who heard Christ's call to leave all and follow Him in poverty, obedience and obscurity, laying aside all hope of marriage and family life, content to sacrifice things which are in themselves good in order that out of the sacrifice some even better thing might be born. They were the stuff out of which came recruits for the monastic life.

THE EVANGELICAL COUNSELS

The three fundamentals of the monastic life, called the "evangelical counsels", are poverty, chastity and obedience: poverty in the sense of having nothing of one's own; chastity in the sense of giving up once and for all the possibility of marriage; obedience in the sense of the complete surrender of one's will to God, which normally implies (as a means to this end) obedience to one's superior in the monastic life. Obviously it would be neither possible nor desirable for every Christian to be a monk or nun. In primitive days it was difficult enough to live one's life as a Christian without there being any incentive to escape from "the world" in order to concentrate upon the Christian virtues. No doubt Christians first fled into the desert to escape from persecution, and not because they had any idea of becoming solitaries or monks. But they did realize, as did St Paul (1 Cor. 9. 24–27), that just as athletes need to train, so do Christians. And they took the Greek word *askēsis*, which means "training"—the training of the athlete or warrior by restraint and exercise—and applied it to the training of the Christian by self-discipline, fasting and prayer. We still use the word asceticism, which comes from *askēsis*, and means living a hard and sternly disciplined life and abstaining from material pleasures and enjoyments.

THE FLIGHT TO THE DESERT

The persecutions under Decius and Valerian, in the middle of the third century, both affected Egypt, and it was then that Christians in Egypt first fled to the desert. Most of them, very naturally, returned to their homes when they could; but they had made the discovery that they could support their life on very little, while the contemplation of God was more possible in the desert solitudes than amid the distractions of the city. So, when they might have returned, some stayed. The first ascetic to make his home in the desert is believed to have been Paul the Hermit, who fled to the desert at the age of sixteen during the Decian persecution and spent the rest of his life (and he was over a hundred when he died) in the Eastern desert between the Nile and the Red Sea. It is amazing how long these desert solitaries lived in spite of the terrific austerities which they practised. St Antony, most famous of them all, is said to have lived to be a hundred and five. Before Paul the Hermit died St Antony visited him and Paul gave him his tunic, made of palm leaves stitched together, which afterwards St Antony was to wear on festivals. Again, when we hear of Paul the Hermit living in a cave before which a palm tree grew, we are reminded of St Antony and how he and the other desert solitaries lived in caves and old pagan tombs (which might have a chamber inside once used by the pagan priests for the rites of the dead) and places like disused forts; and how they supported life on bread (with a little salt) and a few handfuls of dates and water. But Egyptian monasticism was never a thing exclusively of the desert. There were many hermits living close to the villages, and later on there came to be monasteries in the towns as well as groups of monks in little villages of cells on the desert edge. The Nitrian desert, which became alive with monks, was not very far from Alexandria. It was the minority of hermits who sought the greater solitude of the "inner desert", between the Nile and the Red Sea.

ST ANTONY

St Antony himself began by living as a hermit for fifteen years near his own village, first of all going to hermit after hermit, all more or less close by, for instruction in the hermit life. He was born about 250 of a prosperous family at Qoman in middle Egypt, but both his parents died when he was eighteen. Six months later, hearing in the Gospel for the day the words, "If thou wilt be perfect, go, sell all thou hast, and give to the poor; and come, follow me, and thou shalt have treasure in heaven," he obeyed quite literally. He sold all he had, put his sister in a community of virgins (the first of which we hear— she later became its head), and set out to lead the hermit life. After the fifteen years spent near his own village, he moved to a disused hill-fort at Pispir, by the Nile, in the heart of the desert, where food was brought to him twice a year. He would

41

eat only once a day—a little bread and salt—after sunset. Often he spent the whole night without sleep, watching in prayer. People outside would hear him call out, "Let God arise and let his enemies be scattered." He was, as the athlete of God, contending with the hosts of Satan. When he slept it was mostly on the bare ground.

When he was a little over sixty he moved from Pispir further into the Eastern Desert, nearer the Red Sea, where the monastery of St Antony still exists. Here he occupied a cave on the face of a precipice. Pispir was now used to accommodate disciples who had flocked to be instructed by the saint and every few weeks he would visit them. Three times, we know, he visited Alexandria: once, during the last persecution, when he ministered to Christians in prison; then, in 338, to stand by his friend St Athanasius; finally just before his death. For the last fifteen years of his life two monks lived with him.

THE COMMUNITIES: PACHOMIUS

The hermits lived either as solitaries, or in groups of twos and threes, or else in "lauras", little villages of cells. They made palm-baskets and wove linen, and this meant that some of them had to have contact with the outside world—to go to the villages, sell their products and make their own simple purchases. But they did grow a few things themselves such as millet and beans and a little corn, no easy matter in the desert. And on Saturdays (the Sabbath) and Sundays those who lived in the lauras came together for their common worship. Mostly, we must remember, they were laymen; even St Antony was a layman. They depended on those who were priests for the ministering of the Sacraments. Otherwise they lived the same kind of life, each in his own separate cell, spending his days reading, praying, singing psalms (they knew the Psalter by heart and some of them said the whole of it every day), and making their palm-leaf baskets and other simple things.

Even St Antony came to see that monks (even hermits) need to come together, and are the better for being under the authority of an old and experienced monk or abbot. The abbot, as the name implies (Aramaic, *Abba*, "father") is the father of the community. These monastic colonies in the desert came to have their abbots and to agree to a close conformity of life. Then a further important development took place. A former soldier in the army of Constantine, Pachomius (292–346), who had been converted by the kindness shown him by Christians, after living for some time as a hermit, founded a monastery at Tabennesi, on the Nile in the far south. This was a kind of walled city enclosing separate buildings, each containing perhaps forty monks and each under their own provost. Pachomius lodged his monks in separate houses according to their trades (and here he allowed a much wider variety than St Antony, who permitted little besides basket-making and linen weaving): so we find weavers in one house, under their own provost, matmakers, tailors, carpenters, shoemakers in other houses, each with its own provost. So great was the reputation of Tabennesi that Pachomius organized eight other monasteries, of a similar kind, near by, and his sister established two communities for women. The Pachomian monasteries owned two boats which took their goods all the way to Alexandria.

THE MONASTIC RULE

A further development took place when hospital monks were established in Alexandria, to perform works of mercy in the poorer quarters of the city. St Basil (330–79), who became Bishop of Caesarea in Cappadocia, and who visited the monks of Egypt and Syria and Mesopotamia—for the inspiration of the desert spread quite soon far beyond Egypt—made the hospital, the almshouse and the school invariably a part of his monastic establishments. The communities which he set up in Asia Minor south of the Black Sea, were much smaller than those of Pachomius, with no more in the entire community than Pachomius would have had in one of his separate houses; and they were always close to a town. St Basil had seen the harmfulness of sheer individualism and of making asceticism an end in itself, with monks trying to set up records in the austerities they endured or the number of prayers they said. The most famous example of individual asceticism is St Simeon Stylites (388–460), who lived after St Basil's day, and spent the last thirty years of his life on a pillar, a yard across, which was lengthened from time to time until finally it was sixty feet high. That was at Antioch. Even before taking to his pillar Simeon had practised other eccentricities: for ten years he had chained himself to a rock. Syria was apt to produce eccentrics: there were other stylite saints, who lived on pillars, besides Simeon, though none obtained his popularity and superstitious veneration; and there were monks called "grazers" because they lived on grass like animals. St Basil countenanced nothing remotely corresponding to conduct of this sort, but one thing he did, which was to have far-reaching consequences. He drew up a Rule for his monks. This Rule has remained the basis of the monastic life in the Eastern Orthodox Church.

The Rule which underlies western monasticism, the Rule of St Benedict, was not drawn up till a century and a half later. This does not mean that monasticism was all this time in appearing in the West. Its introduction owed not a little to the influence of St Athanasius, who spent his first two periods of exile from his see of Alexandria, just before the middle of the fourth century, in the West. In Gaul St Martin founded a monastery at Ligugé, some four miles from Poitiers, about 360, and, after becoming bishop of Tours, a second monastery, Marmoutier, on the banks of the Loire, close to Tours. Near Marseilles in 415 John Cassian, who had been at one time a monk at Bethlehem and had also lived among the solitaries of Egypt, founded two famous monastic establishments, one for men and one for women. Five years earlier, Honoratus, afterwards Bishop of Arles, had founded on the Egyptian model the abbey of Lerins on an island off Cannes. We should particularly notice John Cassian, not only because he deliberately mitigated the severities of Egyptian monasticism, but because the two volumes which he wrote, the *Institutes* (426) and the *Conferences* (429)—in the latter of which he records the wisdom of the monks of the desert—unquestionably influenced St Benedict when he drew up his Rule.

No better introduction to the monks of the desert can be found than Miss Helen Waddell's *The Desert Fathers*. She warns us not to confuse the crazed figures of the decadence with the quiet men who founded the desert Rule. "It is forgotten that inhumanity to one's self had often its counterpart in an almost divine humanity towards one's neighbour. . . . The desert bred fanaticism and frenzy and fear: but it also bred heroic gentleness." Certainly many of the stories and sayings which she translates give ground for her contention that the essence of the desert teaching was that a man should love mercy and walk humbly with men and God. One story only can be given.

"There came three old men to the abbot Achilles: and one of them was ill spoken of. And one of the three said to the abbot, 'Father, make me a fishing-net,' but he refused. And the second said, 'Make it for us, so that we may have something to remember thee by in our monastery.' And he said, 'I have not time.' Then the third, he that was ill spoken of, said to him, 'Make me a net, so that I may have a blessing from thine own hands, Father.' And he straightway answered him, 'I shall make it for thee.'

"Then the first two whom he had refused asked him privately, 'How was it that thou wouldst not make it for us when we asked thee, and yet saidst to this man, "I shall make it for thee"?' And the old man made answer, 'I said to you, "I shall not do it because I have no time," and ye were not grieved: but if I did not do it for this man, he would say, "The old man has heard about me, that I have an ill name, and for this reason he would not make the net": and I straightway set to upon the cord to sooth his spirit, lest he should be swallowed up of sadness.' " [1]

[1] *The Desert Fathers*, pp. 138, 139. The previous quotation is from the introduction, p. viii. In this chapter I have largely followed, with some modifications, my chapter on "The Monastic Ideal" in my book *The Church of the Apostles and the Fathers*.

7

The Nicene Faith

The common expectation among the Jews had been that when
the Messiah came he would be a second David; but a prophecy
of Micah spoke of One "whose goings forth are from of old,
from everlasting" (5. 2). This was the prophecy to which King
Herod was referred by the chief priests and scribes at the coming
of the Wise Men. It implied a greater than David, One who in
the beginning was with God and was God. When we consider
the kind of Person Jesus was and the kind of things He said,
do we wonder that men asked: "Who is this?" "Never man
spake like this man" (Jn. 7. 46). "Come unto me . . . and I
will give you rest" (Matt. 11. 28); "I came out from the Father"
(Jn. 16. 28); "I and the Father are one" (Jn. 10. 30). If our Lord
called Himself, as He did, the "Son of Man" (which was a
Messianic title), it is to be noticed that never once do the writers
of any of the Gospels call Him this when they are themselves
speaking of Him. They called Him "the Son of God" (cf.
Mk. 1. 1). The Gentile centurion at the foot of the Cross said:
"Truly this man was (the) Son of God" (Mk. 15. 29, where the
Greek has no article); and a disciple, after the resurrection,
can say: "My Lord and my God" (Jn. 20. 28). What is most
remarkable of all, perhaps, remembering their Jewish background, with its stress on the One only God, is that immediately
after His ascension His followers prayed to Him, as they did
to the Father, calling Him "Lord" (Acts 1. 24).

The full Christian belief that Christ is the second Person of
the Blessed Trinity is thus embedded in the Bible, but it was
not expressed in so many words until long after New Testament
times. The Council of Nicaea in A.D. 325 marked an important
stage on the way. The Creed accepted at that Council gave
expression to what, it was claimed, had always been the
Church's faith—that Christ in His essential Being belongs to
the One Reality who is God.

Creeds originated in two ways. They were (i) professions of
faith made at baptism, each church having its own baptismal

Creed; or (ii) statements of the Church's faith put out with some reluctance by councils of bishops because it became necessary to repudiate false and dangerous teaching.

THE BAPTISMAL CREED

First in point of time came the baptismal creeds. Before you could be baptized "into Christ" (Gal. 3. 27) or "into Christ Jesus" (Rom. 6. 3), you were required to say something like "I believe that Jesus Christ is the Son of God" (Acts 8. 37 A.V.) or "I believe that Jesus Christ is Lord" (cf. Phil. 2. 11). The earliest baptismal Creed would, then, have consisted of one statement only, an expression of faith in Christ as Lord. At your baptism you became Christ's. But to become Christ's was to belong to the Father and to have received the Spirit. So baptism was "into the Name of", i.e. into union with, the Father, Son and Holy Spirit. The next stage, then, is that we find the three-fold formula of Matt. 28. 19 coming into use as the formula of baptism.

But the use of the three-fold Name at baptism would quite naturally bring with it a three-fold declaration of faith. Such a declaration would have run, "I believe in God; I believe in Jesus Christ; I believe in the Holy Spirit." Or more probably you would have been asked, "Dost thou believe in God? Dost thou believe in Jesus Christ? Dost thou believe in the Holy Spirit?" and each time you would have replied, "I believe." In an earlier chapter the first and third questions from the *Apostolic Tradition* have been quoted in full.[1] The second question went: "Dost thou believe in Christ Jesus, the Son of God, who was born of the Holy Ghost of the Virgin Mary, and was crucified under Pontius Pilate, and was dead and buried, and rose again the third day, and ascended into heaven, and sat at the right hand of the Father, and will come to judge the quick and the dead?" If we begin "I believe" instead of "Dost thou believe" we have almost got the Apostles' Creed as we know it.

The Apostles' Creed is, in its origin, a baptismal creed.[2] But some creeds were, as we have seen, put out by councils, one such being the Creed of the Council of Nicaea. This is in some ways like, but yet is not the same as, the creed which we know as "Nicene"—the creed which is recited in the Holy Communion service.

[1] See p. 113 *supra*.
[2] The tradition that the Twelve composed it is late and groundless, but there is no doubt as to the primitiveness of the teaching which its clauses enshrine.

THE COUNCIL OF NICAEA—ARIANISM

By 325 Constantine had been sole Emperor for not quite two years. More and more since the day in 313 when he had proclaimed protection for all religions, he had shown himself to favour one—Christianity. He saw in Christianity a force which could unite the Empire as nothing else could. But he found Christians divided, so divided that the very stability of the Empire might be threatened.

The trouble began in Alexandria. Alexandria was split into parishes, each under its own parish priest. There were twelve such parishes and one of them was in the charge of Arius, an elderly man who was generally respected but who had a dislike of anything approaching mystery, and who was vain. Probably that accounts for his thinking that he could explain the truth about Christ's Person in a simple way that everyone would understand. What he taught was very far from the truth but yet it seemed the truth to many. Two of his sayings, referring to our Lord, which together sum up his teaching, are: "There was once when He was not," and: "Out of nothing He came to be." Notice that he did not say there was *a time* when Christ did not exist: he taught that the Son was created by the Father before time was—He pre-existed before becoming man—but nevertheless He was a created being and not co-eternal with the Father. He could not, then, be in any true sense God: rather He was a demi-god of a type familiar in Greek mythology—for which reason the teaching of Arius attracted pagans. Its effect could not but be serious for the Faith. Not being God Christ could not reveal God as He truly is. And how could He redeem man? Only a Christ who is truly divine can be our Redeemer. But many people, even bishops, could not see that Arius's views really made shipwreck of the Faith; it seemed to them that he had simplified the Faith, made it easier, and so they welcomed his teaching. And he was an expert at publicity.

The Bishop of Alexandria, Alexander, reasoned with him. Then, in 321, a synod of Egyptian and Libyan bishops deposed him and two bishops who supported him. Arius went to Palestine, then to Nicomedia, where he secured the support of the bishop, and the controversy spread. He returned to Alexandria, which was now in an uproar of controversy. Popular catchphrases were bandied about in the streets; orthodox Christians were made ridiculous on the stage, and Jews and heathen joined in the fun. That is how matters stood when Constantine, in

September 323, became master of the East. He was compelled to step in. What he did was to send the saintly Spanish bishop Hosius to Alexandria with letters to bishop Alexander and to Arius, telling them to settle their differences.

Hosius, however, saw that the dispute was about something which mattered very much, and on his return probably advised the Emperor to summon a council of bishops. This, the first General (or Ecumenical) Council of the Church, met at Nicaea, where Constantine had a summer residence, from the end of May 325 to the end of August. The Emperor arrived early in July and some three hundred bishops attended. Nearly all of these came from the East, only seven from the West, although Nicaea was easy of access from the West, a navigable river linking it to the Propontis. The Pope sent two priests as his representatives. From Egypt with the bishop of Alexandria came eighteen other bishops, but Alexander also brought with him a twenty-eight-year-old deacon named Athanasius. There were no British bishops present, but five bishops came from the frontiers of the Roman Empire or beyond it, including Theophilus, the fair-haired bishop of the Goths (in Dacia, across the Danube), John of Persia and Paul from Mesopotamia. That two of the bishops from Egypt were minus an eye and Paul's hands had been paralysed by hot irons, show that we are still close to the days of persecution.

"THE NICENE FAITH"

The Council, largely persuaded thereto by Athanasius, who although only a deacon was allowed to speak, condemned the views of the Arians and affirmed in unmistakable language that Christ Jesus is "very (or truly) God", "of the being of the Father", or (what meant the same thing) "of one substance with the Father". That is to say, He is the second Person of the Trinity, "God of (i.e. 'out of', 'coming from') God". The "Nicene Faith", as St Athanasius called it, reads:[1]

"We believe in one God, the Father almighty, Maker of all things visible and invisible.

And in one Lord Jesus Christ, the Son of God, begotten of the Father, only-begotten, that is of the substance (Gk. *ousia*, being, essence) of the Father; God of God, Light of Light, Very God of Very God, begotten not made, of one

[1] Its basis was already existing confessions of faith (baptismal creeds), though the phrases named were new.

substance (Gk. *homoousios*) with the Father, by whom all all things were made, both things in heaven and things in earth; who for us men and for our salvation came down and was made flesh, and was made man, suffered and rose again the third day, ascended into heaven, and will come to judge the quick and the dead.

And in the Holy Ghost."

It was concluded by a number of anathemas intended to shut out the leading Arian tenets. "And those who say 'Once He was not', and 'Before His generation He was not', and 'He came to be from nothing' . . . the Catholic and Apostolic Church anathematizes."

The Council condemned Arius and the two bishops who supported him; and then the State stepped in and banished them to Illyricum. It seemed a brilliant victory but in reality the battle for the Faith was only beginning.[1]

ATHANASIUS CONTRA MUNDUM

Alexander was succeeded as bishop of Alexandria by Athanasius; but already an Arian reaction was setting in. Five times during the forty-six years that he held the see St Athanasius was exiled. All sorts of fantastic charges were made against him by his enemies, from murdering a man in order to obtain his hand for purposes of magic—but the bishop produced the man whole and alive!—to hindering the sailing of the corn-fleet from Alexandria to Constantinople. The last was a very astute invention, as the Emperor would be most unlikely to pass over such a charge. So Athanasius was banished to Trier in 336, the year in which Arius died. However, on Constantine's own death the year following he was recalled to his see. Unhappily Constantius, who succeeded his father in the East, and later in the West as well, was an Arian. His attitude to the Church is shown by his own blunt remark to the supporters of St Athanasius, "What I will, let that be accounted a canon" (i.e. a rule of the Church), "either obey or suffer exile with the rest".

[1] Act 3, scenes 1 to 5, of Miss Dorothy L. Sayers' chronicle-play, *The Emperor Constantine*, which give a vivid picture of the Arian controversy and the Council of Nicaea, should be read if possible. Apart from the argument before and in the Council, there is a diverting scene in a barber's shop and a fishmonger's boy who sings snatches of an Arianizing song.

Athanasius's five periods of exile are:

(1) 336–7.   Trier.
(2) 339–46. Rome (three years); Trier. This was the longest period.
(3) 356–62. Egyptian desert, in hiding amongst monks. Once he escaped from troops who surrounded and broke into a church where he was presiding at a vigil service.
> (In 361 Constantius died and Arianism had reached its zenith.)
(4) 362–4.   Egyptian desert, among monks. His boat was met on the Nile by police who asked for news of Athanasius. He said: "He is not far off," and they hurried on upstream.
(5) Winter
   of 365–6. A short period; in Egypt.

Arianism never had an extensive following in the West, and in the East, once the tide turned, it soon died out except in Abyssinia. But even in the West there were few bishops who had the courage to face exile by resisting the Emperor's wishes. For a time it seemed that Athanasius, supported by the monks of the desert, was up against the world. What made things particularly difficult was that many bishops who were orthodox Catholics at heart disliked the word *homoousios*—"of one substance or essence"—in the Nicene declaration of faith. Their objection was founded on its not being a scriptural word. So Council after Council met and Creed after Creed was drawn up to try to find a substitute for the phrase "of one substance with the Father". But in the end it was realized, as Athanasius had realized all along, that nothing else would do. One substitute which was proposed was "of like substance with the Father". This won much favour but it was in fact hopelessly inadequate and very much too vague.

When Athanasius died in 373, the victory was not yet won, but it was not to be long delayed. The Arian collapse within the Roman Empire followed upon the accession of the Emperor Theodosius (379), who was an orthodox Catholic. But although it disappeared within the Empire, Arianism, perhaps because it seemed to make the Faith easier, was to have a strong hold among the barbarian Teutonic peoples—Goths, Vandals, Burgundians, Lombards—who pressed upon its northern borders.

CONSTANTINOPLE—EPHESUS—CHALCEDON

If the first of the ecumenical Councils brought home the truth that Christ Jesus was "truly God", the second ecumenical Council, which met at Constantinople in 381, stated explicitly the complementary truth that our Lord was "completely man". This was in condemnation of the view put out by Apollinarius, bishop of Laodicea, that "God-made-flesh", Christ in His earthly life, assumed a nature "intermediate between

From a German Print (Picture Post Library)

COUNCIL OF CHALCEDON (A.D. 451)

God and man". This Council also plainly stated the Church's belief in the deity of the Holy Spirit. (The extent to which these were Eastern Councils is shown by the fact that no bishops at all from the West attended this one.)

Both these Councils, and those of Ephesus (431) and Chalcedon (451), were concerned with safeguarding what must ever be an essential mystery, that the Christ of the Gospels *is* both God and man. They do not try to explain *how* this can be, they state that it is so. The rulings of the great Councils were aimed against those who, whether in the one direction or the other, failed to hold the balance even. It was possible to overstress the humanity of Christ. Nestorius, the Syrian-born Patriarch of Constantinople, and his followers did this, when they gave to Christ's human nature a "personality" of its own. Their view, which must seem to us very crude, was that in Christ two "persons", a divine and a human, existed side by side, so that at one moment He would act as God and at another as man. This is the view which the Council of Ephesus condemned. But there were those who pressed down the balance as far as possible in the opposite direction. They were the Monophysites, or "one-nature people", who in stressing Christ's deity, denied the perfection and the permanence of His manhood. They said that "the human nature of Christ was absorbed in the divine, as a drop of honey in the ocean". This opinion was rejected by the Council of Chalcedon. The Pope was represented by two legates but his famous letter, known as the *Tome* of Leo, which he addressed to Flavian, Patriarch of Constantinople, who had solicited his support, was received by the Council as embodying the true orthodox doctrine. The definition of faith drawn up at Chalcedon acknowledged that there was in our Lord two natures, both perfect and complete, the human and the divine, yet only one Person, that of Jesus Christ, the eternal Word.

What adds a tragically depressing note to these two fifth-century General Councils, which the West as well as the Orthodox Church in the East accepted, is that each was followed by a schism which has never been healed. The Council of Ephesus was followed by the severance from Catholic Christendom of the Nestorian Christians, otherwise "the Church of the East". The rival Empire of Persia became their stronghold. The Council of Chalcedon led to the splitting off from the main Catholic body of the majority of the Christians of Egypt as well as of some Syrian congregations. The Armenian Church also threw in its lot with the Monophysites.

THE "NICENE" CREED

It remains to say a word about the Creed which we to-day call the Nicene Creed. At the second session of the Council of Chalcedon two creeds were recited one after the other. The first was "the Creed of the three hundred and eighteen" Fathers of Nicaea—that is, the "Nicene Faith" which has already been set out in this chapter. Immediately after this "the Creed of the one hundred and fifty" Fathers of Constantinople was read, and those present declared: "This is the faith of all, this is the faith of the orthodox; this we all believe." Unfortunately the acts of the Council of Constantinople have not been preserved, but there is no reason to doubt that the Creed which was read at this point at Chalcedon did once occur in them. But for two omissions—"God of God" is omitted, and so too is the phrase "and the Son" after "who proceedeth from the Father"[1]— and not more than one or two minor changes, e.g. "from the heavens" instead of "from heaven", this Creed is the Nicene Creed as we know it—except, of course, that being a conciliar Creed it is in the plural, "We believe . . ."

The Nicene Creed "stands alone among creeds" because it is the only Creed that has ever been recited in the Eucharistic worship of the Church, and it is the only Creed which has behind it the authority of a General Council. It first found its way into the Eucharist at Antioch, not long after the Council of Chalcedon. Early in the sixth century it was in use in Constantinople. Before the century ended it had got to Spain. Rome, always conservative, did not insert a Creed into the Mass until 1014, but it was the Nicene Creed which was then inserted. In Eastern Orthodoxy it is the only Creed that is ever used publicly. Quite early it superseded all local baptismal Creeds in Greek-speaking Christianity, and it has remained in the Orthodox Church the sole baptismal Creed.

[1] On the latter insertion, later on, see below, ch. 14.

To Many Peoples of a Strange Language

ULFILAS AND THE GOTHS

It was the Teutonic tribes nearest to the Roman Empire who first became Christian. Goths, whose old home had been on the Vistula, south of the Baltic, now occupied the whole area between the Baltic and the Black Sea, but in 325 only those living near the Danube were Christians. Ulfilas—his name in Gothic was Wulfila—was then a boy. He was the son of Christian parents and was born in Gothic territory. When he was about twenty he came to Constantinople and there, some ten years later, he was made a missionary bishop for the Goths north of the Danube. For seven years all went well. His preaching won many converts. Then there was persecution, and it was in order to escape that the Emperor allowed him to lead his converts across the Danube into Roman territory, into what is now Rumania. That was in 348. It was thirty years later that Gothic horsemen rode down the Roman legions in the awful battle of Adrianople, destroying two-thirds of the army, with the Emperor Valens. But the new Emperor, Theodosius, induced the Goths to enter his service and with their help became ruler of the whole Empire, East and West. Ulfilas died in 381, while on a visit to Constantinople, after being a bishop exactly forty years.

His great work was to give his people a translation of the Bible, the first in any Germanic tongue. English belongs to the West Germanic group of languages; Gothic, though no one speaks it now, belonged to the East Germanic. Both have a common ancestor. So it is interesting to look at the Lord's Prayer (Matt. 6. 9–13) as Ulfilas translated it from Greek, and to pick out words which are something like ours. Pronounce *q* like *qu*; *gg* as *ng*; *b* between vowels like *v* (cf. *ubils*, evil). In *iu* the stress is on the *i* and the diphthong is rather like the *ew* of *new* in northern English. Gothic had no short *e*, therefore any

55

e (e.g. *Amen*) is a long vowel; the sound of *ay* in *bay* will do for it. þ is here printed as *th*.

"Atta unsar (Father our) thu in himinam, weihnai (be hallowed) namō thein.

Qimai (come) thiudinassus (kingdom) theins. Wairthai (become, be done) wilja theins, swē (as) in himina jah (also) ana airthai.

Hlaif (loaf) unsarana thana sinteinan (literally, our the daily) gif uns himma daga (on this day—a dative case).

Jah (and) aflēt (off-let, i.e. forgive) uns thatei skulans sijaima (what owing we are), swaswē jah (as also) weis aflētam thaim skulam unsaraim (the debtors our).

Jah ni briggais uns in fraistubnjai (temptation), ak (but) lausei uns af thamma ubilin; untē (for) theina ist thiudangardi (kingdom) jah mahts jah wulthus (and might and glory) in aiwins (in eternity). Amēn."

Ulfilas was an Arian but his missionary labours were very far from being in vain. The Goths who took and sacked Rome under Alaric in A.D. 410 were Christians, if imperfect Christians, and they had learned to respect Christian churches. Thousands of pagans owed their lives to taking refuge in one or other of Rome's churches. But this was thirty years after Ulfilas's death.

DIVISIONS OF CHRISTENDOM

We saw that in the middle of the fifth century there occurred a splitting off from the main body of the Church of Christ—Catholic Christendom—of certain bodies of Christians, the most important being Churches in Syria and in lands east of the Roman Empire, and the Coptic or native Church of Egypt. No doubt there were dogmatic differences, but, given good-will, it seems inconceivable that these could not have been mended; and they probably would have been. But good-will was conspicuously absent. Roman, i.e. Byzantine, rule was not popular either in Syria or in Egypt, a fact for which heavy taxation largely accounted, while to the East the Persian Empire was at this time Rome's only rival. There were many Christians in Persia but they were a minority and once Persia's deadly rival, Rome, became officially Christian all chance of Persia also becoming Christian vanished. We can see how it would be likely to make conditions easier for a Christian minority within the Persian Empire if the Church to which they belonged were not in any way connected with the Church of the Roman Empire. Politics, alas, do come in.

Nestorianism, forbidden within Roman territory, became entrenched within the Persian Empire, and there were quite early Nestorian and Monophysite Christian settlements in Arabia, along the trade routes. The most important was at Najran in South Arabia. Syria had many Monophysite Churches— Jacobite Churches as they came to be called after the name of a Monophysite bishop of Edessa who organized them into a powerful body. The Copts of Egypt were inside the Roman Empire for a long time after the Council of Chalcedon, but they were intensely nationalist and for that reason apt to magnify differences rather than try to heal them. The Orthodox Church, of course, existed in Egypt, as it did in Syria and Palestine, but the name given to its adherents, Melkites, "Emperor's men", shows the rather scornful attitude of the native majority. The Catholic or Melkite church was the church of the imperial administration.

THE COPTS

It is said that out of every fifteen or sixteen Egyptians to-day, now of course mostly Moslems, one will be a Copt. The Copts have in fact tried valiantly to keep the Faith which they held when they were part of the undivided Church, and though they speak Arabic, like other Egyptians, for their worship in church they still use the ancient Coptic tongue, the tongue of the Pharaohs, as they did in the days of the Councils.

It is not easy to find a Coptic church in Old Cairo, although there are lots of them. The reason is that they were built *not* to look like churches, and they never have more than one rather furtive entrance. They are churches built by a people in hiding, who did not want their Moslem rulers to know where their churches were. Once inside a Coptic church you would see that its plan is very similar to that of the Roman basilica, though at the far end there would be three altars in a row. The Copts never celebrate at the same altar more than once on the same day, so on great festivals they use three altars, beginning with the middle one. But a Coptic church has two rows of pillars like a basilica, and a space at the back where the catechumens once stood. The altar, too, stands forward as in the old days, so that you could walk round it, and the sanctuary is separated from the rest of the church by a screen. This hides the sanctuary now much more completely than it once did. Coptic altars are made of stone and in them there is a little cavity where the cross is buried every Good Friday on a bed of rose leaves, to be

57

taken out on Easter morning. At the time of the consecration a deacon stands at the back of the altar, facing the celebrant, and looking down the church. He is the look-out man, posted there to give warning of an attack—the practice goes right back to the days of persecution. Another ancient practice is the use of glass chalices. This may be owing to a church being too poor to buy silver, but it continues a custom which is known to have existed in the first century. Yet another link with the distant past is the fact that Copts make their communion standing. They stand for the prayers and usually stand throughout the long services. But one custom—now also found in the Eastern Orthodox Church—is different from the early practice. Communion is administered in both kinds together in a silver spoon. With the Copts the breads used have to be specially baked in the church's own little bake-house on the very morning of the celebration.

In Mr H. V. Morton's *Through Lands of the Bible* a whole chapter is devoted to the Coptic churches of Old Cairo, which he visited in the nineteen-thirties. At the celebration of Holy Communion which he attended—the Copts call it *Korban*—the priest, after making his own communion, went straight to a baptistry, where a three-months-old baby girl was waiting to be baptized. There were two anointings and then the priest grasped the naked infant "firmly by the nape of the neck with his left hand while with his right he held together the left wrist and the left ankle"; then he plunged the infant into the cold water as far as the waist, saying in Arabic (used here because everyone would understand it) "Sabaat is baptized in the name of the Father. Amen." Of course, the baby screamed! Next time the immersion was to the neck—"in the name of the Son. Amen." The last immersion was over the head—"in the name of the Holy Ghost. Amen." Then followed what was in fact the child's confirmation.[1] The priest anointed her with chrism, breathing upon her and saying, "Receive the Holy Ghost." This, as in early days, was followed by first communion. She was too small to be communicated in both kinds at once from a spoon; what the priest did, while the mother dressed the child in a new white dress, was to return to the altar, bring the chalice to the baptistry, and with his finger drop one drop of wine on the baby's tongue. He then splashed water into Sabaat's face (not water from the font), making her gasp, and "in opening her

[1] As in the Orthodox Church the priest is allowed to confirm, using chrism blessed by the bishop.

mouth to cry, she received her first communion". She would not receive her second communion until she was a biggish child. The priest went back to the sanctuary and continued the Communion service to the end.

THE CHURCHES OF THE EAST

There were, as we have seen, many Christians in Persia at the time when the Church there became Nestorian. There had long been flourishing Christian Churches in Mesopotamia and Persia, particularly in the valley of the Tigris. Most of the adherents to Christianity were of the merchant or artisan classes, and a good many were government officials. Soon after the adoption of Christianity by the Roman Empire, Persian Christians endured forty years of vigorous persecution (339–79), and there was persecution sporadically afterwards, even after the recognition of the Christian Church, in 410, as a *melet*, a protected subject community, "a little state within the State". Their patriarch was made responsible for the conduct of Christians and for the collection of their taxes. The Nestorians of Persia very early developed wide missionary interests, particularly in the lands further East—Turkestan, India, and even China. They also had some churches in Syria and Egypt until within the seventh century, when the rise of Islam and its rapid expansion brought a new situation. The Nestorian missions followed the line of the overland trade-routes, and particularly between A.D. 600 and A.D. 800 there was much missionary activity. But the expansion had begun much earlier. There was a bishop at Merv, west of the river Oxus, in 334, and, from Merv, missions went to the south and east of the Caspian Sea as well as the lands further east.

The following localities should be noticed for their Christian associations.

i. *The Tigris Valley*. Ctesiphon, the Persian capital and the seat of the patriarch (called the *Catholicus*); Baghdad, Takrit, Mosul, Nisibin (where there was a famous theological school) were all important early Christian centres.

ii. *The Caspian and Aral Seas and the river Oxus*. There were many Christians on both banks of the Oxus. Merv and Samarqand were the seats of bishoprics. Islam was not a serious rival to Christianity in this area till the ninth century.

iii. *Lakes Balkash and Baikal*. These come in the story rather later. There were strong Christian centres south of the

former from the ninth to the eleventh centuries and some
Christians there up to the fourteenth century. About
A.D. 1000 a mass conversion of a Turkish tribe—the
Keraits—south of Lake Baikal, took place and two centuries later they were still Christian. In this case Christianity spread to the countryside, but in Central Asia and
the Far East this was most unusual. Christianity was in
fact confined almost exclusively to the towns along the
trade-routes.

iv. *China.* Christianity reached Hsianfu (Changan), then the
capital of China, in 635. This date is recorded on a monument set up not quite one hundred and fifty years later,
which says that it was introduced by a Syrian whose name
is given, in Chinese guise, as A-lo-pen. While the reigning house was favourable, as in the eighth century,
Christianity flourished. There were monasteries as well
as Christian churches, perhaps as many as forty. Christianity is known to have reached the coast towns though
it is not known whether it reached Korea or Japan. But
it remained the religion of the foreign trader and made
little headway with the native peoples, who were already
attached to one or other of three advanced religions,
Confucianism, Taoism and Buddhism. Islam arrived in
China later. After 843, when an edict banned all monasteries, whether Buddhist or Christian, the reigning
emperors withdrew their support and Christianity collapsed. In the Middle Ages it was again introduced and
became widespread, only again to disappear in the fifteenth century. Now it has been introduced again; will
it again disappear in the twentieth century?

v. *India.* There was a Christian Church on the Malabar
coast from early times. It became Nestorian; later, towards the end of the seventeenth century, it threw in its
lot with the Jacobite (Monophysite) Church of Syria. A
reformed section of this Church—the Mar Thoma Syrian
Church of Malabar—now claims to have removed all
traces of its past heresies and to be fully Catholic.

In the seventh century the Middle East came under Moslem rule. The Moslem advance into central Asia began a century
later. The river Indus was crossed in 711 but this first incursion
into India proved abortive; the Moslem conquest of northern
India came in the thirteenth century. Eventually it was Islam

which displaced Christianity in the Middle East and in central
Asia, as well as in Syria and Egypt and on the north African
coast. The almost complete wiping out of the once great
"Church of the East" (the Nestorians) by Tamerlane in the
fourteenth century, until only a few remnants were left—the
Assyrians, whose later history was to be so tragic, and who
took refuge in the mountains of Kurdistan—is a story of ruthless conquest; but long before this, and by peaceful persuasion
and not by the sword, the Moslems had made great inroads.
Why should this have been?

In areas where Christianity had remained the religion of the
foreign merchant, the obvious reason is that it collapsed because
it had failed to attach itself to the soil. But this was not true in
the case of either Syria or Egypt and North Africa, where at
the time of the Moslem invasion the bulk of the population was
undoubtedly Christian. Many Christians nevertheless became
Moslems, though by no means all of them did. Even at the time
of the Crusades there were Syrian and Palestinian towns, under
Moslem rule, which had a larger Christian than Moslem population. In Egypt, however many fell away, there were sufficient
native Christians left for the Coptic Church to continue, as
it does to this day. And there were Orthodox Christians too.
Two points will bear pondering over:

i. Christians, like Moslems, believed that the favour of God
was shown by worldly success—and the Moslems were the
conquerors.[1]
ii. Besides its social advantages to one living in an Islamic
State, Islam could be made to appear to those whose
version of Christianity was essentially a simplification of
Catholic beliefs and practices, as a yet further simplification—even possibly an advanced form of Christianity.
Whatever the reason, the Orthodox Christians in Moslem
lands stood firm in proportionally much greater numbers
than either the Jacobites or the Nestorians.[2]

It is humiliating, but it must be stated, that generally speaking
Christians in the East preferred being under Moslem rather
than Byzantine (which was Christian) rule. There were restrictions—one of them forbade a Christian to ride a horse—but

[1] Cf. L. E. Browne: *The Eclipse of Christianity in Asia*, p. 184.
[2] This is shown to have been the case by S. Runciman in *A History of
the Crusades*, vol. i., p. 23.

when Christians suffered it was rather from mob violence than State persecution. Life was seldom made intolerable for Christians in Moslem lands until the Seljuk Turks emerged as conquerors on the wider field of history in the eleventh century.[1]

[1] Latourette, *op. cit.*, vol. ii, ch. 5, and L. E. Browne, *op. cit.*, ch. 7, have been drawn on extensively in the last section.

9

Islam

"On a February day in the year A.D. 638 the Caliph Omar entered Jerusalem, riding upon a white camel. He was dressed in worn, filthy robes, and the army that followed him was rough and unkempt; but its discipline was perfect. At his side was the Patriarch Sophronius, as chief magistrate of the surrendered city." In response to his request, "the Patriarch took him to the Church of the Holy Sepulchre. . . . While they were in the church the hour for Moslem prayer approached. The Caliph asked where he could spread out his prayer-rug. Sophronius begged him to stay where he was; but Omar went outside to the porch of the Martyrion, for fear, he said, lest his zealous followers might claim for Islam the place wherein he had prayed. And so indeed it was. The porch was taken over by the Moslems, but the church remained as it had been, the holiest sanctuary of Christendom."[1]

Jerusalem had been under siege for more than a year; there was no Christian army nearer than Egypt, and food was almost at an end. So the patriarch had gone out, under a safe conduct, to the Mount of Olives to hand over the city to the Caliph himself—the second Caliph or successor to the Prophet of God. This one incident during the first amazing period of Arab and Islamic expansion is worth recalling because it may help to explain why the conquered bore so little resentment to the conquerors. When a Persian army, only twenty-four years earlier, wrested the Holy City from Imperial Rome, churches and homes were burned and sixty thousand Christians massacred. It was very different with the Moslem conquests. Even more astonishing than their speed was their orderly character. "Some destruction there must have been during the years of warfare, but by and large the Arabs, so far from leaving a trail of ruin, led the way to a new integration of peoples and cultures."[2] Christians, Jews, Zoroastrians (most Persians were

---

[1] S. Runciman: *A History of the Crusades*, vol. i, p. 3.
[2] H. A. R. Gibb: *Mohammedanism*, p. 4.

63

Zoroastrians), were all alike regarded as "the People of the
Book", and allowed to practise their religion if they paid the
jizia or poll-tax. In the Arabian peninsula pressure was no
doubt brought to bear on Christians to embrace the faith of
Islam, which would account for the decline of the Christians
of Najran to a tenth of their number within eighty years of
Mohammed's death in 632; but, in general, there was no persecution, no forced conversion. Even after the Christian remnant
in Najran had been removed to new lands in Iraq, there still
remained, so it would seem, some Christians in South Arabia
within the next century.

THE ARAB CONQUESTS

Within ten years of the Prophet's death not only Roman Syria
and Egypt but Iraq and almost the whole of the Persian Empire
had been conquered. Thanks to the barrier provided by the
Taurus mountains, Asia Minor still remained to the Roman
Empire. Even allowing for the fact that the nineteen years of
struggle between Persia and Rome (only over in 629, when
Heraclius celebrated the restoration of the lost provinces to the
Roman Empire by a triumph in Constantinople), had left both
Empires much weakened in their capacity to resist, the Arab
conquests are amazing. In 649 Cyprus was in Arab hands.
Before the end of the century they had taken Carthage and,
just after the turn of the century, had not only broken the resistance of the Berber tribes of the Barbary coast but won them for
Islam, so that they joined in the Arab invasion of Europe,
where they landed at Gibraltar in 711. Within four years the
conquest of Spain was almost complete, though the remnants
of a Christian army held out in the far north, in the Asturias.
And not only did they hold out, but in 718 won a victory over
the Moslems; which indeed marked a turning-point. However
the victorious march was not yet halted; the Moslems crossed
the Pyrenees in 720 and did not withdraw into Spain until their
defeat between Poitiers and Tours by Charles Martel, son of
King Pepin of Burgundy, in 732. This was exactly a hundred
years after the death of Mohammed. By this time they were in
Turkestan, preparing to advance into Central Asia; in the year
when they landed in Spain they had made their first incursion
into India; and before A.D. 800 they were in Zanzibar.

The first great age of Islamic expansion lasted for a century.
It was followed by an age which saw the development of a new
and splendid material civilization, which reached its climax in

Paul Popper, Ltd.

THE KAABA AT MECCA

The congregation of pilgrims dispersing after prayers. Here is the centre of the Islamic faith

(See page 65)

From the picture by Blaas ("*Picture Post*")

CHARLEMAGNE, EMPEROR OF THE WEST.
Long before becoming Emperor in A.D. 800 he made Alcuin of York Master of his Palace School.   (See page 112)

the ninth and tenth centuries, when the seat of the Caliphs was at Baghdad. For a while Cordova vied with Baghdad in prosperity and splendour—until the reconquest of Spain by the Christians in the middle of the eleventh century. When, in 1502, Ferdinand and Isabella gave the Moslems of Spain the choice of baptism or expulsion, Islam had been in Spain for eight hundred years. On the whole both sides were tolerant, and Christians and Moslems lived side by side.

MOHAMMED (571–632)

What do we know of Mohammed, but for whom there would have been no Islamic faith? Not very much, in fact, is known about his life. He was forty when he was called to be the Prophet of God; a Meccan proud of his city and no Arab of the desert, whose journeys as a merchant had brought him into contact with both Jews and Christians. The religion which he preached was certainly influenced by ideas derived from both Christianity and Judaism. "Earlier scholars postulated a Jewish source with some Christian additions. More recent research has conclusively proved that the main external influences (including the Old Testament materials) can be traced back to Syriac Christianity."[1] Professor Tritton, who says that Mohammed's debt to the Bible is obvious, thinks that his religious life may have been started "by suggestions received from outside the Arab circle of ideas. He took stories from both Testaments to illustrate and enforce his ideas about God, providence and the last judgement."[2] Belief in one supreme God, Allah (Allah=The Deity), seems to have been common ground between himself and his Meccan opponents, whose religious observances yet found a place, as his did not, for many idols. Even if his belief in the One God did not come from the Bible—the Biblical stress on the one true God and its hatred of idols would have impressed him.

Modern Islamic scholars warn us to accept with great caution the stories about the Prophet; but one is worth recording. It seems that when he was in his middle thirties the Kaaba at Mecca was rebuilt. This is a cube-shaped building (Kaaba means "cube"), which it was claimed that Abraham and Ishmael had originally built. Who should place in position the "black stone" (built into the east corner breast high from the ground) which it was said that Gabriel had brought from Paradise? Because the Kaaba contained this stone, Mecca was

---

[1] Gibb, *op. cit.*, p. 37. [2] A. S. Tritton: *Islam*, p. 20.

already the centre for pilgrimages before the Pilgrimage to Mecca was erected into one of the Five Pillars of the Islamic religion. It seems that Mohammed was chosen to lay the stone because he was the first to enter the court of the Kaaba by a certain gate. Did he, who was in the habit of keeping long night watches in prayer, ask himself why God had chosen him for this honour?

But in any case he had no idea at first of preaching a new religion. He recalled his fellow-citizens to the worship of Allah, and he held before them continually the terrors of the Last Judgement. This last was certainly derived from Christian sources. "The profound disbelief and scornful sarcasm with which it was received by his Meccan fellow-citizens show that it was a wholly unfamiliar idea to them."[1] There is no doubt at all that Mohammed was sincere, and that he believed that the revelations handed down in the hundred and fourteen *suras* or chapters of the Koran (Arabic, *Qur'ān*, the Reading) were genuine revelations, which he had received, when in a condition of trance, from the angel Gabriel, whom he thought to be the same as the Holy Spirit. Zaid bin Thabit collected the oracles of Mohammed into a volume, at the command of the first Caliph, Abu Bakr, in the first three years after the Prophet's death. He did not arrange the *suras* chronologically or according to their subjects, but according to length. The longest are placed first, the shortest last. They are, of course, in Arabic, and Arabic is regarded as the language of heaven. For centuries it was thought impious to translate the Koran into any other language. (This stress upon Arabic is important because it meant that the Arab impress upon Islamic culture would remain after the chief centres of Islam—apart from the religious centre—had ceased to be in Arabia.)

At Mecca, however, Mohammed met with disappointment and resistance, and when the people of Medina, two hundred miles north of Mecca, invited him to come there as an arbitrator between rival Arab tribes, he left Mecca secretly and established himself at Medina. That was in the autumn of 622, and Moslems reckon their dates from the *Hijra* or flight to Medina; and because the Prophet entered Medina on a Friday, Friday is the sacred day of the Islamic week.

By this time Mohammed had come to look upon himself as the preacher of a new religion. He was the Prophet of God. God had made His will known through a hundred and twenty-four

[1] Gibb, *op. cit.*, p. 39.

thousand prophets, but of these six, through whom God had introduced a new law, stood apart; Adam, Noah, Abraham, Moses, Jesus, and Mohammed himself. Mohammed reverenced Jesus, and believed in the Virgin Birth, but did not believe that Jesus is divine, nor did he believe that He was crucified. That was a Jewish fable; another in his semblance had been put to death in his place. We should notice that Islam, with its emphasis on Allah the Master and man his slave, has no place for a saviour. But, however much Mohammed was conscious of being the Prophet of God, once established at Medina, where his preaching won greater acceptance, he "could not resist the temptation of securing a worldly kingdom". At Medina the Islamic movement first assumed the form of a community organized on political lines under a single chief. Even in the conditions of those days such a conception was difficult, and in less than half a century the Islamic State and the Islamic Church had become separated. The conditions of our own day may force Islam to adopt the position of a church inside a secular state, but that is not the position the Prophet envisaged. For him Church and State were one, a single community, an indivisible whole.

It may be that Mohammed's character did not degenerate so markedly through the possession of power as used to be supposed, but nevertheless it did degenerate. After some seven years he captured Mecca with little fighting, and at once ordered the three hundred and sixty images of the Kaaba to be destroyed. But he did not stop the pilgrimages, and Mecca, so far from showing the resentment of a beaten enemy, indicated its willingness to become the centre of the new Islamic State. Intellectually and politically Mecca led western Arabia; it was essential that it should take the lead, though Mohammed realized well enough that the real spiritual centre was Medina. But in either case the desert does not come in. Islam is not the religion of the desert. Before he died Mohammed planned nearly fifty military expeditions, and when he died almost the whole Arabian peninsula had accepted Islam. Pagans were given the choice of Islam or the sword but "People of the Book" (and this title, stretched to include the Zoroastrians, was stretched yet further many centuries later, on the conquest of northern India, to cover the Hindus) were left unmolested. Outside Arabia itself, though many Christians fell away to Islam, it was not uncommon to find them employed by the Moslems in official positions. There were many Christian physicians.

SOME IDEAS OF ISLAM

Islam, which is used to denote both the Moslem religion and
the Moslem world, is an Arabic word meaning "submission",
i.e. "to the will of God". Moslem is an adjective from the same
root, and the name chosen by the Prophet himself. Moslems
dislike being called Mohammedans because, they say, the name
suggests that they worship Mohammed in the same way that
Christians do Christ. The Moslem believes that the will of Allah
is made known in the Koran and also in the *Sunna*, the custom
and practice of the Prophet. This has been handed down by
tradition, and the Koran and the tradition are equally binding.
Both, for example, teach the rightness of the *jihad* or holy war,
though we need to remember that one Moslem comment ran:
"The holy war has ten parts; one is fighting the enemies of
Islam, nine are fighting the self." Mohammed however in the
last ten years of his life fought in twenty-seven battles and
promised the reward of Paradise to all who died fighting for
Allah. His example always has counted, and the true Moslem
tries to follow in the steps of the Prophet as the Christian does
in the steps of Christ. We see the influence of the Prophet's
practice in all sorts of ways, even in the characteristic style of
the mosque (mosque="place of prostration"). The first mosque
which Mohammed helped to build at Medina was domed;
therefore most mosques are domed. Mohammed would allow
neither picture nor image; therefore whatever decorative adorn-
ment a mosque may have, you will find no statues, no pictures.

The dome reminds the Moslem of the vault of the sky and
consequently of the One God. Islam finds no place for a Trinity.
What makes a man a Moslem is the recital of the Kalima or
short creed: "There is no God but Allah: Mohammed is the
Prophet of God." Its denial brands him as an infidel who will
be excluded from Paradise. The Koran teaches that God will
judge every man according to his works, yet the Moslem finds
it hard to believe that any Moslem will not enjoy the delights
of Paradise. Most Moslems have regarded them as material
delights but whether Mohammed, who was a mystic, so regarded
them is less certain. Islam has produced a great many *sufis*, as
they call their mystics (the name came from the undyed garments of wool—*suf*—which the early ascetics wore in imitation
of Christian monks), and they have often held very lofty and
spiritual views of religion, including the after life. The resurrection of the body is taken for granted.

In one respect the Moslem can put most Christians to shame: he does not mind being seen praying. Five times a day—before sunrise, at noon, before sunset, at twilight, after dark—the muezzin chants his summons to prayer from the minarets. "God is most great. I bear witness that there is no God but God (Allah). I bear witness that Mohammed is the Prophet of God (Allah). Come to prayer, come to prayer! Come to the Refuge, come to the Refuge! God is most great, God is most great! There is no God but God (Allah)."

Wherever he is at these times of prayer, the Moslem spreads his prayer-carpet on the ground, turns towards Mecca, and recites the set prayers in Arabic. They must be in Arabic for that is the language of heaven; whether he understands or not, does not matter. It does matter, however, that before he prays the Moslem should form the intention of performing a religious act—a safeguard against mere formalism, though Moslems, like Christians, are not immune from this. After the set prayers the Moslem may add others in his own tongue, but petition will be almost wholly absent, since the Moslem believes that everything is already determined by God. The set prayers are accompanied by movements of the body, bowings and prostrations, and these are considered as important as the prayers. If they are omitted the prayers are valueless. Prayer consists for the most part of statements about God or ascriptions of praise to Him. Thus, the ninety-nine names for God are repeated, "the Merciful, the Gracious, the Master, the Holy, the Faithful, the Creator", etc., but they do not include the word Father. To the Moslem the relation between God and man is not that of Father and son; though he is very conscious of a brotherhood of "believers", to which all who will say the Kalima are admitted irrespective of race or colour or anything else. When Berber tribesmen first carried Islam into negro Africa, the Moslem welcomed the negro as a brother, as he does to-day.

The recital of the Kalima; the five official daily acts of prayer; the fast during the month Ramadan (a total fast from food from sunrise to sunset); the giving of alms to orphans, widows and the poor; the *Haj* or Pilgrimage to Mecca (to be made once in a lifetime if possible): these are the "Five Pillars" of religion. The Moslem is not allowed to drink wine, though he will in Paradise (unless he be among those "who do not care for" such things and to whom God grants instead "to look upon His face"). He may have as many as four wives—Mohammed, by a special concession, had ten. Islam raised the position of women among the Arabs, yet all the same woman is regarded as very much man's inferior. At Medina at the beginning, women worshipped in the mosques, standing at the back, but afterwards (until recent times) it was thought better that they should pray at home. The veil, probably not in use at first, soon became almost universal, and Moslem women all through the centuries have worn the veil until our own day; and to-day it is noticeable that the Moslem women, who had discarded it, are wearing it again in Pakistan.

There are many different sects within Islam, though we need notice only one—the Shia sect, now represented by the Moslems of Persia. This began as a political movement among the Arabs themselves in early days, and maintained the exclusive right of the house of Ali, the son-in-law of the Prophet and the fourth Caliph, to the Caliphate. This sect holds that a secret interpretation of the Koran was transmitted by Mohammed to Ali and by Ali to his heir. The Imam, or head of the community, has a spiritual function in the Shia form of Islam which no one person has in orthodox Islam. Islam, in fact, covers a multitude of differences, but in one form or another it is to-day the religion of one-seventh of the estimated population of the world. When in the Indian sub-continent alone there are ninety million Moslems, and in Malaya and Indonesia some fifty-five millions, and upwards of fifty millions in the Arab-speaking world, Islam remains a force which still challenges Christianity, as it has done all through its long history. It is the only religious faith (modern Communism and secularism are not religious faiths although Communism at least has much in common with one) before which Christianity has ever receded in any part of the world. In some parts of Africa it is receding to-day.

10

Monks and Missionaries

IONA

In 1773 not many visitors from England found their way to the
Inner Hebrides. One who did was Dr Samuel Johnson, in company with his young Scottish friend, James Boswell, whose
home was in Ayrshire. They met in Edinburgh, passed up the
east coast to Inverness, then crossed to the west, visiting most
of the islands, including Iona, a tiny island close to Mull, only
three and a half miles long by one and a half wide. The abbey
buildings on Iona had been in ruins since the Reformation. Dr
Johnson said: "That man is little to be envied . . . whose piety
would not grow warmer amongst the ruins of Iona."

When the writer visited Iona in the summer of 1948 there
were still ruins but less of them; to-day there are even fewer.
The abbey church was restored over forty years ago; in 1948
slates and timber were stacked close by the church and the
roof was being put on the building which had been the monks'
refectory. The slates were local, from a near-by island, but the
timber came from Norway, a gift from the people of that
country. A Norwegian who had been there in the war had
interested his fellow-countrymen and they had made the gift
so that they might share in the scheme for the complete restoration of the Abbey buildings. Viking raiders many times went to
Iona to plunder and destroy. Martyrs' Bay, facing Mull, the
little village with the jetty where one lands, is so named because
it was there that sixty-eight monks were murdered on a big
Viking raid just after A.D. 800. Now their descendants have made
an act of reparation. How fitting, too, that Norway should help
with the work of restoration for another reason. For about
three hundred years from 1100, this part of Scotland belonged
to Norway and eight Norwegian kings are buried on Iona as
well as forty-eight Scottish kings (who include Duncan and
Macbeth) and four Irish kings.

It may have been after this big Viking raid that the site where
the Abbey now stands was first built on. St Columba's very

71

simple church and the wattle and daub huts of his monks were half a mile distant. Even before he came in 563 by coracle from his beloved Derry in Ireland, Iona was a sacred isle and one Christian saint (St Oran, died 550) lay buried there. St Columba came with twelve companions (two priests and ten lay brothers), but before he died before the altar of his church on a June Sunday in 597, he had founded more than fifty churches and monastic groups in the north and west of Scotland and the Western Isles.[1] The same year St Augustine landed in Kent.

THE IONA COMMUNITY

The present-day restoration of the Abbey of Iona is the work of the Iona Community, which is a brotherhood, a kind of fellowship (not monastic, for many of the members are married) belonging to the Church of Scotland—which is Presbyterian— whose property the Abbey is. The Scottish Episcopal Church has a house, which is used for retreats and other purposes, on another part of the island. The ministers and craftsmen who make up the community are kept together by a common rule and discipline. In 1948 there were six craftsmen, under whom the ministers worked for the three months of their stay on the island as labourers—though they had their own particular work to do as well, taking services, leading discussions and so on for parties of young people, workers in industry, students from college; indeed all sorts of people come to Iona. Normally it is only for three months in the summer that the community is at full strength on the island; then the young ministers go back to work in Glasgow and other towns and cities. In the winter of 1948–9 the temporary Community House remained open and for the first time all the craftsmen stayed on the island to carry on with their work and continue the regular daily worship. For just as the minister can work with his hands, so the craftsman can lead in worship; and the community believes, as did St Columba, that all life must be offered to God.

ST COLUMBA, ST NINIAN, ST MARTIN, ST PATRICK

St Columba was forty-two when he came to Iona; he had been only twenty-five when he had built his first church and monastic

---

[1] The number has been variously estimated at from fifty to three hundred. Miss Diana Leatham, in *They Built on Rock*, p. 137, says that "he founded a hundred [monasteries] in Ireland and Scotland". This chapter is greatly indebted to her book.

group of cells at Derry—within sight and sound of the sea, for the Celtic saints loved the water. His birthplace was Garten in Donegal and he was a prince by birth. He might himself have been one day High King of Erin but instead he chose the service of God. At nineteen he went to Moville to study under St Finbaɪ, an Irish-Pict, and at Moville he was made a deacon. (Later he became a priest; he was never a bishop.) Finbar, however, had studied at Candida Casa, the White House at Whithorn in Galloway—which St Ninian was building, as we know, in the very year that St Martin of Tours died. That was in 397, exactly two hundred years before the death of Columba, and it is the first known date in Scottish Christian history.

Ninian was British-Roman, a native of Cumberland, who had gone to Rome for training in the days when the Roman Empire was declining and the Christian Church advancing, and it was at Rome that he was consecrated as bishop for the western part of Britain, which as yet knew little of Christ. On his way home he stopped at Tours where St Martin was bishop. Martin, a native of western Hungary and the son of heathen parents (his mother later became a Christian), had wanted from the age of ten to be a monk; but it was not until he was eighteen that he was baptized. He was then a soldier and it was at Amiens, in 334, that he cut his cloak in half to clothe a beggar, and the next night had a vision of Christ wearing the cloak and saying: "Martin, still a catechumen, clothed me with this garment." Since that day Martin, who left the army, had read St Athanasius's life of St Antony, and though he had never been to Egypt, he strove in the communities of monks which he founded at Ligugé and Tours to carry out the ideals of the Desert Fathers. Like St Antony's monks, his monks had their own separate cells, as had those of St Ninian and St Columba. But St Martin added something to the monasticism of the desert. He insisted that the monk can also be a missionary.

From St Martin's monastery on the banks of the Loire, two miles from Tours (where the cells were caves hollowed out of the overhanging cliffs) groups of twelve disciples under an acknowledged leader would go out to found a new monastic house, a new group of cells, a new base for the conversion of Gaul to the Faith. Two other things about St Martin should be remembered: the austerities which he practised; for like St Antony he slept on the bare ground with only sackcloth for a covering; and the fact that the copying of manuscripts was the one art which he permitted to his monks. Even in Scotland St Columba slept on

the bare ground; and no task did he think more important than
the copying of the Scriptures and especially the Psalms. St
Columba himself copied the Gospels or the Psalter more than
three hundred times. He was copying the 34th Psalm within an
hour or so of his death, the last verse which he copied being
verse ten. But St Columba, in fact, felt the influence of St
Martin not only through St Finbar, trained in the tradition of
St Ninian who himself had actually known St Martin and who
modelled his methods on his; but also, before coming to Iona
himself, he had once led a party of pilgrims to the tomb of St
Martin at Tours. So it is altogether fitting that at Iona, not far
from the west door of the Abbey, St Martin's Cross should
have stood since the tenth century.

Another who had found his way to Tours was St Patrick and
it was there that St Patrick first came into touch with monasticism, though he was trained at Lerins, the famous monastery
on an island off Cannes. But, as we have already seen, Lerins
had been founded on the Egyptian model, so all roads were
leading back to the Desert. The year that St Martin died, St
Ninian was building Candida Casa; the year that St Ninian
died (432), St Patrick returned as bishop to Ireland, which he
had left as a runaway slave. Like Ninian he was British-Roman
and had been carried off as a boy to Ireland in a raid on the
British coast organized by Niall of the Seven Hostages, whose
descendant St Columba was.

St Ninian, and St Columba later, followed the same method
as St Martin, sending out parties of twelve with a leader. Nor
were they all priests; mostly they were not; but rather scribes,
smiths, masons, shepherds, carpenters, craftsmen of one sort
or another. Beginning at Candida Casa and keeping to the east
of the Grampians, St Ninian was instrumental in founding a
chain of churches, the farthest north being at Navidale on the
east coast of Sutherland. There were churches at Glasgow, near
Arbroath, at Temple (on Loch Ness), at St Ninian's (south of
Stirling and close to a Roman camp), and elsewhere.

ST PATRICK

From Candida Casa monks did indeed go to Ireland; there
were Christians there before St Patrick's mission. But not much
headway had been made before the return of St Patrick, who
could not rest because of the voice which he heard, "the voice
of those that lived beside the Wood of Fochlut, which is beside
the western sea." Rightly we think of St Patrick as the Apostle

of the Irish. His travels as bishop extended over the whole island except the south-west corner, and everywhere he founded and furnished churches and ordained clergy to serve them. There were churches, to name only a few, at Strangford Lough where he landed (his first convert being a dog that had been set on him, and his second Dichtu the dog's master, his first church Dichtu's barn); at Slane where on his first Easter Eve he lit his Paschal Fire in full view of the High King and the Druids assembled at Tara; at the Wood of Fochlut (where probably he had spent his earliest days as a captive, and up to then—he was fifteen or sixteen at the time—had not thought much about religion, although a Christian); and at Armagh, where he built the cathedral that was to be his see as Primate of Ireland. He died in 461, near the first church which he had founded.

"A CERTAIN GUEST, A CRANE"

From Ireland and from Scotland monks set out to carry the Faith across the whole of Europe. To Lindisfarne, the cradle of our Faith in Northern England, came St Aidan from Iona; and foremost among his Northumbrian disciples was St Cuthbert, born about 634, and dying in 687 as Bishop of Lindisfarne. Cuthbert's body was removed from the church of Lindisfarne during the Danish invasions and after many wanderings found a final resting-place in the church which was the predecessor of the present cathedral at Durham. He was, as Miss Leatham says, "the greatest of English saints in the Celtic tradition," but his life "would have been impossible without the tireless zeal of missionaries from Iona."[1] From Ireland missionaries went to the Shetlands and the Faroes and may even have reached Iceland. They went south too. The monastery of Bobbio in Italy was founded by St Columbanus, who was Irish like St Columba, while Gallus, also from Ireland, founded St Gall in Switzerland. One thing nearly all the Celtic monks had in common with St Francis of Assisi and the Desert Fathers —a love of all dumb creatures. There was the old white horse at Iona which came whinnying to St Columba, pouring out "the tears of his bitter lamentation" just before the saint died. His earliest biographer, St Adamnan—ninth abbot of Iona, who died in 704—tells us about him. But best, perhaps, is Adamnan's story of the crane.

"At another time, when the Saint was living in the isle of

[1] *Op. cit.*, p. 132.

Iona, calling one of the Brethren to him, he thus addresses him: 'On the third day from this now dawning, thou must keep a look out in the western part of this isle, sitting on the seashore; for from the northern region of Ireland a certain guest, a crane, driven by the winds through long, circling aerial flights, will arrive very weary and fatigued after the ninth hour of the day; and its strength almost exhausted, it will fall and lie before thee on the shore, and thou wilt take care to lift it up kindly and carry it to a neighbouring house, and there wilt hospitably harbour it and attend to it for three days and three nights, and carefully feed it; at the end of the three days, refreshed, and unwilling to sojourn longer with us, it will return with fully regained strength to the sweet region of Ireland whence it originally came. And I thus earnestly commend it to thee for that it came from the place of our own fatherland.'

"The Brother obeys, and on the third day after the ninth hour, as commanded, he awaits the coming of the expected guest; and, when it comes, he raises it from the shore where it fell; carries it, weak as it was, to the hospice; feeds it in its hunger. And to him, on his return to the monastery in the evening, the Saint, not by way of inquiry, but of statement, says: 'God bless thee, my son, because thou hast well attended our stranger guest; and it will not tarry long in exile, but after three days will return to its country.' And, just as the Saint predicted, the event also proved. For having been harboured for three days, raising itself on high by flight from the ground in presence of its ministering host, and considering for a little while its course in the air, it returned across the ocean to Ireland in a straight line of flight, on a calm day."[1]

[1] *The Life of St. Columba,* by St Adamnan, tr. from the Latin by Wentworth Huyshe, ch. 48 (pp. 86, 87).

11

The Coming of the English — Bede

Exactly two hundred years separated the death of St Martin, in 397, and the coming of St Augustine, in 597. When St Martin died and St Ninian was at work building the White House in Galloway, the Roman Empire was breaking up. St Patrick was a small boy living with his Christian parents in his British home. The withdrawal of the Roman troops in 407 left the country open to attacks not only by raiders from Ireland but from the Continent as well, where the Teutonic races were on the move. The experience of the ship's crew with whom St Patrick companied when he escaped from Ireland shows what their movements meant. They landed in Gaul to find the whole countryside devastated and no food to be obtained anywhere. The Vandals had passed that way into Spain.

Half-way through the century some Jutes began to colonize Kent and the Isle of Wight and parts of Hampshire. Angles and Saxons followed in their wake. A leader like Hengist, probably to begin with, entered with his retinue into the service of a British king and then, when the time was ripe, revolted. But the invaders did not have it all their own way. About 550 they met with a serious repulse at the Mons Badonicus (Mount Badon). Where this was we cannot be sure; perhaps near Bath, but, anyway, somewhere in the west. Very few people seem to be aware of return migrations, after a British victory, of many of the English back to the Continent. British rule was re-established over much of the island and fifty years later the effect of the British victory had not disappeared. The real King Arthur, the Arthur of history about whose figure legends multiplied, was probably a British leader at the time of this revival.[1]

The Anglo-Saxon conquest and settlement was not, then, immediate. It was spread over a great part of our two hundred

[1] For reasons why Arthur should not be removed altogether from the sphere of history, see Stenton, *Anglo-Saxon England*, p. 3.

years, and was incomplete even when St Augustine landed in Thanet. A British kingdom of Elmet existed right into the seventh century; it stretched westward from the head of the Humber and separated the Angles of the Midlands from those farther north. Of the British some at least were Christians; yet, except in the fastnesses of the west, Christianity disappeared leaving hardly a trace. This may have been because the British Christians kept their Christianity to themselves and did not try to convert their Saxon foes. Later on St Augustine was to find British bishops and teachers, whom he met in conference at a place called "Augustine's Oak", apparently somewhere in Gloucestershire, unwilling to join in preaching to the English nation. We may suppose that the British members of the conference came from South Wales. They went home, leaving St Augustine and his followers to "preach the way of life to the English nation".

The English were heathen, but there is one thing which suggests that their conquest of the Britons was not completely ruthless. There were some church buildings existing, if ruined, which St Augustine could restore. St Martin's at Canterbury, the first church Augustine used, had been partially restored even before his coming; it was the church used by the Christian Queen Bertha, and her chaplain, bishop Liudhad. If you visit it to-day you will see that a considerable section of the chancel is built of Roman bricks, which are long and not very thick. In the south wall of the chancel are two doors: one, which is square-headed, is an original Roman doorway, but the other, which is smaller and round-headed (Saxon arches, like Norman, were round), was probably put in in Saxon times and may have been the one Queen Bertha used. There is a good deal of Saxon work in St Martin's dating from St Augustine's time and later.

One thing the English took from the Celtic Britons was their way of pronouncing "Christ" with a long *i*. They did not bring the pronunciation with them from the Continent, for all other Germanic peoples pronounce "Christ" with the *i* short as in "Christian", just as the Latin races do. It is not as if, in English, we usually have a long *i* before *st*. Think of any words you can—*mist*, *twist*, *list*; no, the long *i* is abnormal and it was taken from Celtic. Apart from what we have seen at St Martin's, Canterbury, our pronunciation of "Christ" is about the one surviving trace of the Church which was here before St Augustine.

78

RELICS OF HEATHENISM

Although the Anglo-Saxon conquest may not have been entirely ruthless the conquerors were rooted in their heathenism. How do we know this? For one thing, there are the names of most of the days of the week—Tuesday (Tiw, the Germanic god of war), Wednesday (Woden's-day), Thursday (Thunor's-day—Thor is the Norse form of the name), Friday (which was named after Frig, the wife of Woden or Odin). The English had taken the names of the days of the week from the Romans, but they substituted their own gods for the classical ones—thus Mars becomes Tiw. (However, they kept Saturn so that we still speak of Saturday.) Then, there are a good many place names which have a heathen origin. Harrow (from O.E. *hearh*, a hill-sanctuary) was originally a heathen centre of worship. A stretch of wooded downland in East Hampshire is known as Wheely Down—Wheely comes from *weoh*, an idol, and *leah*, a grove. *Weoh* is common in English place names—e.g. Wye in Kent. The village of Tuesley (Surrey) has the name of the war-god. Thundersely and Thunderley, both in Essex, go back to the worship of the thunder-god, Thunor or Thor. Wednesbury, in the heart of Mercia, indicates a cult of Woden (Woden's-fortress). Sir Frank Stenton reminds us that such names are largely confined to an area "which can be indicated on a map by lines drawn from Ipswich to Stafford, and thence due south to the Channel".[1] Does this mean that heathenism was strongest in this area? Heathenism did not yield without a struggle. Even in Kent the Church nearly collapsed on the death of its protector, Ethelbert, the first Christian king. His son and successor was not at first a Christian. And London certainly drove out its first bishop, Mellitus, whom Augustine had appointed and consecrated not long before his own death.

THE SUTTON HOO SHIP-BURIAL

The English might be heathen but they had a culture of their own; discoveries like that made at Sutton Hoo in Suffolk (between Woodbridge and the sea, nine miles from Ipswich), in the summer of 1939, make this plain.[2] The discovery was of a ship eighty-five feet long and fourteen feet across at its widest

[1] *Op. cit.*, p. 102.
[2] I am heavily indebted to the March 1940 number of *Antiquity* for the account that follows.

point, buried deep in wet sand and full of the most costly and exquisite treasures; sword and sheath, shield, helmet, spearheads, chain mail, a purse with a golden frame and set with jewels (it measured seven and a half inches in length and contained forty gold Frankish coins), a large gold hanging bowl with magnificent mosaic glass adornments, a small five-stringed instrument of a kind probably used by a *scop* or bard to emphasize the points of his song, remains of fabrics, a nest of nine small silver bowls, a large silver dish with stamp marks on it dating from Anastasius I, an emperor who ruled at Constantinople from 491 to 518, and many other things, including two silver spoons, ten inches long, with a cross and the names Paulos and Saulos respectively inscribed on the handles, just above the bowl. These inscriptions almost certainly refer to St Paul the Apostle and the spoons will have come from a Christian source. Such treasures can have belonged to no one but a king; a heathen king, for no Christian king would have looked with favour on such a burial.

When, we may ask, was the ship taken on rollers across country from the river Deben to its place of burial not far from the residence of the East Anglian kings at Rendlesham? From the objects found one can say, not before A.D. 600 nor after 650. Probably 625 will not be far out. The king commemorated will then probably be Redwald of East Anglia, who succeeded the Christian Ethelbert of Kent as Bretwalda or chief-king. Redwald had been baptized when on a visit to Ethelbert but his wife was fiercely heathen and persuaded him to revert to heathenism on his return home. He died about 624–5, possibly away from home; which would account for the fact that there is no trace of a body ever having been buried in the ship. A special chamber to house the treasure, seventeen and a half feet long, with a gable-ended roof, was built on the ship, making it look like a Noah's Ark. This structure collapsed long ago under the weight of the wet sand and all the woodwork has completely disappeared.

We should notice both the great wealth here brought together, and the artistic quality of many of the objects. The gold ornaments are of English workmanship, with intricate and unusual designs. The silver objects probably came from the eastern Mediterranean; the large silver dish clearly came from Constantinople. These might have been gifts but are more likely to have been acquired in the ordinary course of trade (not plunder). There was commerce between England and the Continent and strong links between the English reigning houses and the Franks.

There is an account in *Beowulf*, the splendid epic which the English brought with them from beyond the seas (it is about Denmark and southern Sweden, but was not written down till long after our ancestors came to this island) of a heathen ship-burial, which reminds us of what was found at Sutton Hoo, except that the body of Scyld is placed on board the ship and the ship then set adrift.

> They then him bore to the ocean's wave,
> His trusty comrades as he himself bade,
> Whilst with words ruled the friend of the Scyldings (i.e. the Danes),
> Beloved land-prince; long wielded he power.
> There stood at haven with curved prow,
> Shining and ready, the prince's ship:
> The people laid their dear war-lord,
> Giver of rings, on the deck of the ship,
> The mighty by th'mast. Many treasures were there,
> From distant lands, ornaments brought;
> Ne'er heard I of keel so comelily filled
> With warlike weapons and weeds of battle,
> With bills and burnies! On his bosom lay
> A heap of jewels, which with him should
> Into the flood's keeping afar depart:
> Not at all with less gifts did they him provide,
> With princely treasures, than those had done,
> Who him at his birth had erst sent forth
> Alone o'er the sea when but a child.
> Then placed they yet a golden standard
> High o'er his head, let the wave bear
> Their gift to the sea; sad was their soul,
> Mourning their mood. Men indeed cannot
> Say now in sooth, hall-possessors,
> Heroes 'neath heaven, who that heap took.[1]

The jewels and the treasures, the bills and the burnies (coats of mail), this might be Redwald's ship—if the Sutton Hoo ship be Redwald's. His ship, however, had no mast; it had once been rowed by thirty-eight rowers.

[1] *Beowulf*, ll. 28–52, in J. M. Garnett's line-for-line translation (Ginn). The translation keeps close to the original; Old English verse did not rhyme but used alliteration.

THE VENERABLE BEDE

However, when the Sutton Hoo ship was lowered into its carefully prepared grave the days of heathenism in Anglo-Saxon England were numbered. Kent was already Christian; it was nearly thirty years since St Augustine landed and twenty years since his death. In 625 Paulinus, one of his followers, set out for Northumbria, and two years later in the first wooden church at York, the earliest St Peter's, Edwin of Northumbria was baptized. But behind St Augustine's mission was a greater than himself, St Gregory, rightly called "the Great".

That we know so much about these early days of Christianity in this country is due almost entirely to the Venerable Bede, who carried his *Ecclesiastical History of the English Nation* (written in Latin), down to 731, four years from his death. And he really did know what he was writing about. Of that so great an authority as Sir Frank Stenton leaves us in no doubt. "Bede was in touch with men who could have told him much about the origins of the English kingdoms. . . . In view of Bede's relations with the Northumbrian court, it is highly dangerous to reject anything that he offers as a statement of historical fact."[1]

Nearly everybody knows—or used to know—the story of Bede's death: it comes from the account of an eye-witness, Cuthbert, writing to a friend. He was taken ill towards the end of Lent, but was able to go on instructing his pupils at the monastery at Jarrow and translating part of St John's Gospel. On the Tuesday before Ascension Day he was worse, but all the Wednesday morning he spent in translating. In the afternoon he gave such little gifts as he possessed ("I have in my chest paper, napkins and incense") to his brother monks. "In the evening his boy-scribe said to him: 'One sentence, dear master, is left unfinished.' He bade him write quickly. Soon the boy announced that it was finished. 'True,' the dying man said, 'it is finished. Take my head between thy hands and raise me. Full fain would I sit with my face to my holy oratory, where I was ever wont to pray, that sitting so I may call on my Father.' And so he sat on the floor of his cell, and chanted 'Glory be to the Father and to the Son and to the Holy Ghost.' And as he breathed the words 'the Holy Ghost' he died."[2] Ascensiontide had begun with Vespers of Ascension Eve.

[1] Stenton, *op. cit.*, p. 8.
[2] G. F. Browne: *The Venerable Bede*, pp. 14, 15.

Bede himself tells us the few facts we know about his life in the last chapter of his *History*,[1] where he also gives a list of his writings. About the time of his birth, which was in 673, a Northumbrian noble, Benedict Biscop, had founded a monastery at Wearmouth (at the mouth of the Wear, now Sunderland). Here, at the age of seven, Bede was placed under the charge of its founder and abbot. Biscop was full of enthusiasm;

Picture Post Library

THE VENERABLE BEDE (673–735)

ECCLESIASTICAL HISTORIAN

not satisfied with Wearmouth he persuaded the Northumbrian king, Ecgfrith, to give him some more land for a second monastery. This was at Jarrow, on the south bank of the Tyne. It was finished in 682, and among the first to be transferred there was Bede, as a boy of nine. Though we know of visits to Lindisfarne and to York, Bede hardly ever left the monastery. Benedict

[1] There is a translation in the *Everyman* series.

83

Biscop, however, paid many visits abroad, several to Rome, and always brought back manuscripts, pictures, statues, vestments, for his twin monasteries of Wearmouth and Jarrow. He even brought back with him John, the chief cantor of St Peter's, Rome, to teach his monks to sing the services properly. Bede tells us he loved the singing in church, but also he "always took delight in learning, teaching and writing." We owe him an immense debt for his *History*.

Bede was a monk and a priest; but he is always called "the Venerable". Probably it was just a title of respect; Bede himself speaks of Benedict Biscop as "the Venerable Benedict". Afterwards, the title was accounted for in a number of ways, which are usually miraculous. One story says that, being blind (we have no reason to think that he was) and preaching to a congregation which did not exist, the angels answered his prayer, "Amen, Venerable Bede." Another story makes a disciple halt for the right word to put before his name in composing his epitaph; next morning he finds the blank filled in presumably by angelic hands with the word "Venerable"—*Hac sunt in fossa Bedae Venerabilis ossa* ("In this tomb are the bones of the Venerable Bede."). These words are to be found on Bede's tomb now in the Galilee chapel of Durham Cathedral.

12

The Conversion of the English

THE ROMAN MISSION

St Gregory would have liked to come himself. But he was called to do other work. As Pope, it was he who chose Augustine, the prior of his own monastery of St Andrew on the Coelian Hill at Rome, to lead the enterprise, and it was he who urged the monks forward when, on hearing such dreadful accounts of the English as they passed through southern Gaul, they wanted to turn back. And when Augustine returned to know whether they need "undertake so dangerous, toilsome and uncertain a journey", Gregory did two very wise things. He gave him immediate authority by making him abbot (if the mission went well he was to return to the Continent for consecration as bishop); and he gave him letters of introduction both to the bishop of Arles (the chief bishop of Gaul, who later consecrated Augustine as bishop) and to one or two Frankish kings through whose lands the mission would pass. These Frankish rulers were Christians. The Christian queen Bertha, wife of Ethelbert of Kent, was the daughter of Charibert, the Frankish king of Paris. His son-in-law, Ethelbert, though not a Christian, was almost bound to give a friendly reception to visitors coming with Frankish recommendation. Gregory, it is interesting to notice, wrote a personal letter to Queen Bertha—which Bede unfortunately does not give us—telling her she ought to have done more to convert her husband.

Ethelbert received Augustine and his companions ("nearly forty men", Bede says) sitting in the open air; he felt safer out-of-doors, fearing magic! Though not immediately won to the new faith, he allowed the monks to settle at Canterbury, supplied them with food and allowed them to preach. They drew near to the city singing a litany; their first church was, as we saw, St Martin's. Here, afterwards, Ethelbert was baptized. The seal of St Augustine's Abbey, built in honour of St Peter and St Paul outside the city walls at Canterbury, is dated 1280, and shows Ethelbert being baptized in a font similar to that

85

which still exists, and which is certainly a Saxon font; though the Normans made it taller by inserting a tier of different design just below the rim. Whether this tub-shaped font is the actual original or not, it is nevertheless very early. It is made of twenty-two separate pieces of Caen stone.

When the king had been baptized the monks were able to build or repair other churches and many converts were made. Little was attempted outside Kent in Augustine's lifetime: a mission to London, under Mellitus, consecrated bishop for the East Saxons, was not a success, though the first St Paul's goes back to this time.

St Augustine died probably in 604, in the same year as St Gregory. Something of Gregory's keen interest in the mission to England is shown by the long and patient answers which he gave to Augustine's enquiries about how he was to govern the newly-founded Church.[1] The answers show that the Rome of Gregory's day was not hide-bound in its rigidity. For example, Augustine had asked why, since the Faith was one, there were different customs in different churches, particularly in the manner of celebrating Holy Communion. Gregory replied that even though Augustine had been bred up in the customs of Rome, yet if he found anything in the Church of Gaul or any other church which might be more acceptable to God, he was to teach it to the English. He was to choose those things which were pious and right, draw up a body of rules for the English Church and accustom the people to them. If others had had the wisdom of Gregory, the differences which tended to separate Roman and Celtic Christianity would more easily have been resolved.

ROMAN AND CELTIC CHRISTIANITY—NORTHUMBRIA

The setting up of the first Christian Church in Northumbria sprang from the Roman mission. Paulinus went to Northumbria, accompanying the Kentish bride of King Edwin—daughter of Ethelbert and a Christian—in 625. In 627 Edwin was baptized at York, and a rapid extension of Christianity followed. But this did not go very deep; the Church collapsed in 632, when Edwin was slain by the heathen king of Mercia, Penda, who had, alas, Christian allies from North Wales. Paulinus fled, taking back with him to Kent the widowed queen. He became bishop of Rochester and never returned to the north. However,

[1] See Bede, *Hist.*, Bk. I, ch. 27.

the year after Edwin's death a new Christian king was established in Northumbria, Oswald, and thanks to him the Christian religion was re-introduced. He however did not look to Canterbury but to Iona, where he had spent some time as an exile. From Iona St Aidan came, to make his centre not at York (as Paulinus had done) but on the tidal island of Lindisfarne off the Northumbrian coast. This he made a second Iona and it came to be known as Holy Island. Here he established a monastery on the simple and austere lines of St Columba's Iona, and from there he made his missionary journeys on foot up and down the land. Aidan was a most attractive character. This time the roots went deep; within twenty years the north was firmly established in the Christian faith.

But its Christianity was derived through Iona from Ireland; Celtic customs were followed, some of which were different from those of Rome. In particular the Celtic and the Roman churches differed as to the date of keeping Easter. This did not matter so long as the two Churches were out of contact with each other; but it became a pressing problem once they were in close touch. We can appreciate the difficulty felt by king Oswy of Northumbria, who would be keeping Easter according to the Celtic use, while his wife, a Kentish princess, brought up in the tradition of Rome, was still keeping Lent with her chaplain and attendants. It was Oswy who, in 633, presided over a synod held at Whitby in Yorkshire, where the question was settled in favour of the Roman use. Wilfrid, the young abbot of Ripon, put the case for the Roman usage with characteristic fervour. He had returned to Northumbria, after studying at Rome and Lyons, full of enthusiasm for Roman ways. Actually his claim that the Roman date for Easter went back to St Peter was quite unhistorical (so indeed was the Celtic claim that their date went back to St John); but it was in fact important that one date should be observed by the whole church in the country, and also important that the Church in England should not cut itself adrift from the rest of the Catholic Church.

One of those present at the synod of Whitby was St Hilda, the famous head of the abbey of Whitby—which was a double monastery, i.e. a monastery for monks and nuns, who each had their own separate parts. A double monastery always had an abbess at its head. It was to this monastery, in the days of St Hilda, that there was attached a shy and retiring cowman, whose name we all know, because he was the first English poet —Caedmon. Probably only one short poem that he wrote

87

survives, a poem in praise of the Creator, beginning (it is, of course, in Anglo-Saxon):

> Now should we hymn the warden of heaven's kingdom,
> The might of the Maker and the thoughts of his heart.

ENGLAND RECEIVES THE FAITH

It is useful to notice (i) the regions which owed their Christianity to Lindisfarne; (ii) to Canterbury or Rome. In both cases a great part was played by missionaries from other lands. The Church of England was a *receiving* Church.

Indebted to Lindisfarne were:

(*a*) Mercia (the Midlands). Peada, the son of the heathen Penda, became a Christian and was baptized by St Aidan's successor (Finan) at Lindisfarne. His father allowed him to introduce four priests into Mercia. He got them from Lindisfarne. One of them, an Irishman, Diuma, was Mercia's first bishop. And Mercia's most famous early bishop, the humble and saintly St Chad—who built the first cathedral at Lichfield— had been trained and consecrated at Lindisfarne.

(*b*) Essex. The first bishop consecrated for Essex was St Cedd, an older brother of St Chad (there were four brothers who all became priests and two of them bishops). Cedd had been one of the four priests introduced by Peada into Mercia, and when appointed bishop had gone not to Canterbury but Lindisfarne for consecration. However, he and his brother Chad both fell into line about the Roman date of Easter.

Indebted to Canterbury or Rome were:

(*a*) East Anglia. It was the Archbishop of Canterbury who consecrated St Felix, a Burgundian, to be the first bishop. He had his seat at Dunwich, now under the sea.

(*b*) Wessex. Here Birinus (possibly an Italian, certainly foreign) was sent direct by Pope Honorius. Agilbert, the next bishop, was a Frank. The see was at Dorchester on the Thames until the seizure of West Saxon lands north of the Thames by Mercia caused its transference to Winchester about 676.

A RECEIVING CHURCH—THEODORE OF TARSUS

Whether from Ireland (through Iona and Lindisfarne) or from the Continent and Rome, Christianity was introduced to England by foreign missionaries. We should note the double strain —Celtic and Roman. Celtic Christianity was full of missionary zeal; it produced saints, Christians of great humility and real holiness, but it lacked order. The Archbishop of York has said that "the bishop is first and foremost the pastor of the flock" but he is also "the overseer of his diocese". A Celtic bishop like Aidan was undoubtedly the pastor of the flock, but the Roman bishop was more than the Celtic the ruler of a diocese. What was necessary was that the two strains should be blended together. This was done by a Greek monk living at Rome whom the Pope made Archbishop of Canterbury in 669. He was Theodore of Tarsus, St Paul's birthplace. It was a very bold appointment, for not only was Theodore an old man (sixty-six when appointed and sixty-seven when he got here) but he had been bred in the traditions of the East. He lived to be eighty-eight and was one of the greatest archbishops England has ever known. (He came to be sent because the priest chosen in England and sent to Rome for consecration died there of plague before he could be consecrated; whereupon the Pope decided that he must select a successor, and chose Theodore.) Bede said of Theodore: "This was the first archbishop whom all the English Church obeyed." A modern historian has said, "If any one man was the founder of the English Church, it was Theodore"[1]: he made the Church one whole. But we were still a *receiving* Church.

WILFRID AND THE CONVERSION OF THE SOUTH SAXONS

The time was soon to come when we should be a *giving* Church. As early as 677 one Englishman, Wilfrid, now Bishop of York, spent a whole winter in Frisia (Holland) preaching daily to the heathen and making many converts. But converts need building up in the faith, and Wilfrid was merely passing through Frisia on his way to Rome. Twelve years later no traces of his labours seem to have been left. Wilfrid was going to Rome to appeal to the Pope against Theodore's action in dividing into four his diocese of York, an enormous diocese, stretching from the Humber to the Forth. No doubt it did need dividing and Theodore, knowing that Wilfrid might prove difficult, did so without consulting him. The Pope ordered his reinstatement as bishop of the complete diocese, but on Wilfrid's return he found himself thrown into prison by the Northumbrian king; he was later released and banished from Northumbria. He went to Sussex. The South Saxons living there were the last people of the mainland to remain heathen. The reason possibly was that Sussex was cut off from the rest of the country by forests and

[1] Hodgkin, *History of the Anglo-Saxons*. p. 310.

Romney Marsh. Wilfrid won the Saxons for Christ, doing a magnificent work among them, and teaching them how to increase their food supplies by fishing. He established a monastery at Selsey and Selsey was the bishop's see until just after the Norman Conquest, when it was transferred to Chichester. Before Wilfrid left Sussex, Christianity had been carried from Selsey to the Isle of Wight. After five years Wilfrid was recalled to the north and reconciled with Theodore; and as the king who had banished him was now dead, he was restored to part of his former diocese (Hexham and York).

13

Boniface — Alfred — Dunstan

This chapter is mainly about three very great Englishmen—St Boniface, King Alfred and St Dunstan. From St Boniface's birth in 680 to St Dunstan's death in 988 is roughly three hundred years. And they were not years of steady and peaceful development.

A GIVING CHURCH

We have seen how soon, both in Ireland and Scotland, the Celtic Church became a *giving* Church. England was in fact *the* mission field of the Celtic Church of Scotland, though not the only one, and some monks from Ireland came here too. The Anglo-Saxon Church similarly began to send out missionaries to the Continent of Europe. We have seen that St Wilfrid spent a winter in Frisia on his way to Rome. But when other missionaries went to Frisia in 690, twelve years afterwards, they found a completely heathen people. This time the leader of the mission was a priest from Northumbria, Willibrord, who had eleven lay monks with him. After five years the Pope made him a bishop. But at this time the Frisians were struggling to be independent of the Franks, and even in southern or Frankish Frisia the position of the Church was not very secure. There were many set-backs, and once Willibrord had to retire from his see of Utrecht; but he returned and for three years (719–22) had as a companion a Devon man, Winfrith of Crediton, better known as St Boniface, for whom Mr Christopher Dawson has made the tremendous claim that he had a deeper influence on the history of Europe than any other Englishman who has ever lived. Willibrord lived long after Boniface left Frisia; he died as a very old man in 739 after having been a missionary for nearly half a century.

ST BONIFACE, THE APOSTLE OF GERMANY

Boniface, who came from a monastery near Southampton, set out from England with his abbot's blessing in 716. But fighting was going on between Franks and Frisians and missionary work was at a standstill. He returned to England. Two years later he was abroad again, bearing letters from the Bishop of Winchester to the Pope. The Pope gave him authority to "hasten to any peoples . . . held in the errors of unbelief", to preach to them and baptize them. It was then that he rejoined Willibrord in Frisia. But he wanted to make Christians of those who had been completely untouched; he therefore left Willibrord and went to Hesse and Thuringia, where he made many converts. The Pope made him bishop for the whole of Germany east of the Rhine. Here he later established eight bishoprics and founded many monasteries, the most famous being Fulda. It was at Fulda that he was buried. For nearly forty years he laboured, evangelizing the heathen often at the risk of his life; and though he went on preaching tours on foot like a Celtic bishop, his aim was to set up an ordered Church in communion with Rome.

Many Englishmen helped him, some becoming bishops. There were Englishwomen also. When he was getting an old man he wrote to his cousin Leofgyth or Leoba, who was a nun at Wimborne in Dorset, asking for her prayers that his work in Germany might not be fruitless. A year afterwards she set out, with a party of twelve nuns from Wimborne and twelve monks from Malmesbury, for Mainz, of which place Boniface was now archbishop. She became the head of a double monastery for monks and nuns in Baden (Tauberbischofsheim). It may be an over-bold statement that without Leofgyth "St Boniface could not have gained the proud title of 'The Apostle of Germany'", but he owed her and her nuns an enormous debt. She too was buried at Fulda.

Two incidents illustrate the courage of St Boniface. In his earlier days he cut down with his own hand, in full view of the heathen, the great "Thunderer's Oak" sacred to Woden, and with the timbers built a little wooden chapel out of which grew the church and monastery of Fritzlar (in Hesse). The other incident is his martyrdom, when he was perhaps nearer eighty than seventy. He never forgot Frisia, where he had first laboured, and northern Frisia was still largely heathen. So he went back there with a company of priests and teachers in 754. On Whitsunday (June 4th) they were all gathered at Dokkum awaiting the arrival of some newly-baptized converts whom Boniface was to confirm, when a band of heathen attacked them. St Boniface forbade resistance. "Cease, my children, from conflict.

Lay down the purpose of battle . . . Fear not them who kill the body, but cannot kill the soul." Fifty companions died with him.

ALFRED OF WESSEX

We must skip a century and come back to England, and to Alfred, born at Wantage in 849 and dying in 899. The Danes had long before this begun their raids on our shores. (The Norwegians, who attacked Scotland and Ireland, and who had before 800 destroyed the church at Lindisfarne and Bede's old monastery of Jarrow, mostly left England to the Danes, at least until after Alfred's day.) In 835 the Danes sailed up the Thames, and ravaged the island of Sheppey. They came, at first, to plunder, not to stay, but even so they could disembark a force of five thousand men. Kent suffered most.

In 850, when Alfred was one year old, a Danish force wintered in England. But in 851, Aethelwulf of Wessex, Alfred's father, won a victory somewhere south of the Thames over an army comprising three hundred and fifty ships' companies, who had previously burnt Canterbury and stormed London. The same year Athelstan, under-king of Kent, defeated the Danes at sea, off Sandwich, in the first naval battle recorded in English history. Alfred was later to be called the Father of the English Navy because he built ships to fight the enemy at sea. This was the high tide of the Viking invasions, when the Norsemen even sailed through the Mediterranean sea to besiege, though unsuccessfully, Constantinople (865). It is not surprising that the English in their battles with the Danes did not always come out victorious.

In 871, when Alfred was twenty-three, he became king of the West Saxons. Nine inconclusive battles had been fought between the Wessex men and the Danes, in some of which Alfred had taken part. Perhaps the invaders now sought an easier prey; at any rate, Alfred was able to conclude a peace with them by which they agreed to withdraw across the Thames. Already East Anglia was Danish, and they had established themselves in York. They now overran Mercia, though the western part of that country suffered comparatively little. Learning could still be found in Worcester when the great fenland monasteries, Crowland and Ely, had been destroyed. In 876 Halfdene, the Danish leader, dealt out at York to his followers the old kingdom of Deira "to plough and till", and about the same time Mercia received Danish settlers. They set up five centres, called the Five Boroughs (from *burh*, a fortified place), at Lincoln, Stamford, Nottingham, Derby and Leicester. This is the part of England, along with Yorkshire, in which the Danish influence took deepest root. Life must have been pretty grim for the English in those days.

In 875 the Danes renewed sea-raids on Wessex, attacking Poole and Wareham. Then, when a Danish force which had taken Exeter was compelled to capitulate and it might have seemed that Wessex was safe, a new Danish leader named Guthrum who had been in Cambridge, overran Wiltshire in the winter of 877, almost taking Alfred by surprise at Chippenham, where he was keeping Christmas. This was the blackest period of all. Alfred had to retire to the marshlands of Somerset. The Easter following he stockaded himself in the isle of Athelney with a few followers; then, in May, he put himself at the head of the men of Somerset, Wiltshire and Hampshire and met and defeated Guthrum at Edington near Westbury. From now on the danger to Wessex ceased, and the Mercians, whose king had been a puppet of the Danes, offered Alfred allegiance.

Guthrum retired to East Anglia, but he did so as a Christian whose godfather Alfred had become. The baptism was at Aller near Athelney; after it Guthrum stayed with him twelve days. It had been a condition of the peace concluded at Chippenham that Guthrum should be baptized. This may seem odd to us, yet it speaks volumes for the wisdom and the faith of Alfred, and for the vitality of the Anglo-Saxon Church, that the Danes were so soon won over to the Christian faith.[1] In the main their conversion seems to have been genuine. Before very long they were themselves sending missionaries to Scandinavia with names such as Sigurd, showing that they came from the Danelaw. "In saving Wessex, Alfred saved England, and in saving England saved Europe from becoming a heathen Scandinavian power."[2] Alfred deserves to be called "the Great!"

HIS REFORMS

Alfred was great in other respects too. With the coming of peace he introduced naval and military reforms, in particular establishing a chain of some twenty-five fortified strongholds (Hastings, Southampton, Exeter, Bath, Southwark and others). But his heart was set on other reforms. He wanted to secure just

[1] McLeod Campbell: *Christian History in the Making*, p. 18.
[2] C. Plummer: *Life of Alfred*, quoted by McLeod Campbell.

treatment for all his people, a project needing just laws and their observance. He revised the laws of earlier kings and added a few of his own. But what he tried hardest to do was to revive religion and learning.

He began as a learner, so that he could himself read and translate Latin. To help him, and to give to the people the most necessary knowledge in their own tongue, he drew to his court scholars like the two Mercians, Waerferth, Bishop of Worcester and Plegmund who became Archbishop of Canterbury, and the Welsh Asser, from St David's, who afterwards became Bishop of Sherborne and wrote Alfred's *Life*, and two monks from the Continent, one of whom he made abbot of a monastery he founded at Athelney. With their help a number of works were turned into English (i.e. Anglo-Saxon), for example, the *Pastoral Care* of St Gregory the Great (this was to help the clergy), Bede's *History* and Orosius's *History of the World*. Orosius is rather dull but Alfred added to the book something that is anything but dull, the voyages of two travellers who had visited his own court. One was Ohthere, whose home was within the Arctic Circle and who claimed to have been as far as the White Sea. "Ohthere said to his lord, Alfred (the) king, that he dwelt northmost of all Northmen. He said that he dwelt in the land to the north by the West-sea. He said though that the land extends very far north thence; but it is all waste, except that in a few places here and there Finns dwell, (engaged) in hunting in winter, and in summer in fishing by the sea." This was good, interesting talk, of the reindeer and the northern moose and the walruses. "This whale is much smaller than other whales," Ohthere says, and he brought some tusks for the king, adding that walrus-hide made excellent ship-ropes. The other traveller was Wulfstan, who had sailed from Slesvig to near the Vistula. Alfred plainly enjoyed meeting men like these.

The preface which he wrote for the translation of St Gregory's *Pastoral Care* shows how desperately education was needed. "Alfred (the) king bids greet Waerferth (the) bishop with his words lovingly and with friendship; and I bid to be made known to thee that it has very often come into my mind what wise men formerly were throughout England, both of sacred and secular (orders); and how happy times there were then throughout England; and how the kings who had the power over the people in those days obeyed God and his messengers; and how they maintained peace and morality and order at home and extended it abroad; and how it succeeded with them then both in war and wisdom . . . and how abroad one sought wisdom and learning hither in (this) land, and how we now must procure them abroad if we would have them. So completely was it (learning) fallen off in England that there were very few on this side of Humber who could understand their mass-book in English or even translate one letter of Latin in English; and I ween that there were not many beyond Humber. So few of them were there that I cannot think of one single one south of Thames when I came to the throne. Thanks be to God Almighty that we now have any supply of teachers."

It was Alfred who set on foot the *Anglo-Saxon Chronicle*, and who may well have had a hand in composing the stirring record of the last years of his reign when fighting had once more broken out. Picture him, old at fifty, working in his palace at Winchester long into the night at this and other tasks. One thing he never forgot, his devotions. Half his time and half his income he gave directly to the service of God.

REVIVAL COMES: ST DUNSTAN

With conditions so bad it was too much to expect a big improvement immediately. The decline had been too great. It had affected all classes. But fifty years or thereabouts after the king's death a marked improvement began.

First had to come more settled conditions. Alfred's son, Edward the Elder, extended his rule to the Humber, but Athelstan, after the battle of Brunanburh, near the Solway, 937, could put on his coins *Rex totius Britanniae* (King of all Britain), and twenty years later Eadred was ruling the entire country to the Forth. In particular the reign of Edgar (959–75), a great supporter of the Church, was one of peace. It is true that in 980 the Danish raids began again and ended only when Cnut became king of the whole island (1017–35), but Cnut was a devout son of the Church (he had been baptized in Germany) and the England he ruled over was a Christian land.

There is an early rhyme, known as King Cnut's Boat-Song, which goes like this:

> Merie sungen the muneches binnen Ely
> Tha (when) Knut king rew therby:
> Roweth, knihtes (row, boys), ner the land
> And here we thes muneches sang.

And the king did enjoy listening to the monks' chanting. But that Ely and other great religious foundations had been rebuilt and were now again the homes of monks, who lived strict lives and followed the monastic Rule of St Benedict, was due to the good use made of the earlier period of peace, and especially to St Dunstan.

Dunstan (924–88) belonged to a noble family connected with the reigning Saxon house. As a boy he had spent some time in the monastery at Glastonbury, near his home; but the monks had kept no proper Rule. After a period at court, he had himself resolved to become a monk, and while still very young was made Abbot of Glastonbury. There he was able to introduce reforms. The monks now had to live as monks, to sleep in a common dormitory, to eat at a common table, to keep all the times of prayer. Dunstan was already devoted to learning, to music, to the making of lovely illuminated manuscripts, and to metalwork; and Glastonbury soon became a home of all these arts. From Glastonbury this better state of things within the monastery spread to other foundations, when monks trained under Dunstan were appointed as abbots. Some became bishops. Dunstan himself was made Archbishop of Canterbury in 960 and then he was able to help on the revival of religion outside as well as inside the monastery.

There may be, not far from where we live, a church some part of which was built in Anglo-Saxon days. If so, it will probably date, at least if we are outside Kent, from the century after St Dunstan, the last before the Norman Conquest, when there was much church building.[1] The Anglo-Saxon Church of this period, as Sir Frank Stenton has convincingly shown, has in the past been much maligned; it was in fact no whit behind the Church in other parts of Europe. We see here the fruits of the earlier reforms, as we do also in the West Saxon version of the Gospels (995). The translation was well done and was probably in wide use. Here is the Lord's Prayer as given in St Matthew, chapter 6. The Anglo-Saxon þ (thorn) has been printed as *th*. Short æ is pronounced like *a* in *hat*, long ǣ like *ai* in *air*; final *e* is pronounced.

"Fæder ūre thu the eart in heofonum, sī (be) thīn nama

[1] The map in T. D. Atkinson's *Local Style in English Architecture*, p. 45, shows that the number of churches containing some Saxon work is considerable. They may not contain much—the church at Hinton Ampner is shown but only three pieces of Saxon work survive, a small round arch, two pilaster strips, and a very little long-and-short stonework. All these are typical Saxon features. But the little Saxon church at Corhampton, only a few miles away, really is in the main a Saxon church. Both probably date from the late period.

4   97

gehālgod (hallowed); To-becume (come) thīn rīce (kingdom); gewurthe (be fulfilled, be done) thīn willa on eorthan swā swā (as) on heofonum; Ūrne dæghwāmlīcan hlāf (our daily loaf) syle (give) us to-dæg; And forgyf us ūre gyltas swā wē forgyfath ūrum gyltendum (our offenders); And ne gelǣd thu us on costnunge (temptation) ac (but) ālȳs (loose) us of yfele. Sōthlīce (truly, i.e. Amen)."

Unlike Ulfilas's Gothic the West Saxon version does not contain "For thine is the kingdom, etc.". The reason is that the Saxon scribe translated, naturally enough, from the Latin Vulgate, which does not contain the addition, whereas the Greek text, which Ulfilas had before him, did.

14

Rome Constantinople and the Orthodox Church

ST SOPHIA

The church of the Holy Wisdom, Sancta Sophia (a designation of our Lord), was the loveliest and most wonderful church in Christendom. According to Procopius, who saw it when it was first built, it seemed "to be suspended by a gold chain from heaven". The West had nothing to compare with it. The Emperor Justinian had it built and the building took five years (532–7); its two architects, who deserve to be remembered, were Anthemius of Tralles and Isidore of Miletus. The enormous dome, one hundred and seven feet in diameter, rests on four arches which in their turn are supported by four colossal piers. There are two semi-domes which come just below the central dome and lean against its great arches. The design was inspired by the great domed buildings of Persia, which existed before Mohammed, as of course St Sophia did. Mohammed borrowed the dome as he borrowed much else, and made it a characteristic feature of the mosque.

Looked at from outside St Sophia is a magnificent structure; inside it must originally have been breath-taking in its loveliness. The screen, the altar and the pulpit were all adorned magnificently with silver and gold. The light screen, which divided the sanctuary from the rest of the church, did not completely separate the two parts of the building as the *iconostasis* of an Orthodox church now does. The sanctuary could be seen. Then, too, there were many-coloured marbles "so skilfully variegated as to give an illusion of oriental carpets," dazzling mosaics on a background of blue and gold, lofty columns with exquisite capitals. Think of it with its candles, its clouds of incense rising from the censers of the sacred ministers, its choirs singing unaccompanied music (to this day instrumental music is not permitted in Orthodox churches), its stately processions and splendid ceremonial. It is no wonder that it seemed to the

99

ambassadors of Vladimir the Great, Grand Prince of Kiev, that the angels were descending from heaven to join with the priests in celebrating the Liturgy. Such were the reports which they carried back that their master decided to seek baptism and to seek it from Constantinople. And he let his people know that he expected them to be baptized too. It was with this mass baptism of Vladimir and his people in the river Dnieper in A.D. 989 that the Church in Russia began. Its centre remained at Kiev until that city was sacked by the Tartars in 1240, when it moved northwards, to become established at Moscow towards the close of the Tartar period in the fourteenth century.

THE LITURGY

The Russians of Vladimir's court who were entranced by the splendour of St Sophia, had been unimpressed by the Roman Mass. The simpler worship of the Roman West in no way appealed to them. There was a difference then between the Liturgy (the Orthodox name for the Eucharist) and the Mass, the eastern rite being then, as it is to-day, the more elaborate; yet fundamentally the two services were the same.

The Liturgies of St Chrysostom and St Basil in use in Constantinople in A.D. 600 are still those principally used by Orthodox Christians to-day. They are much alike, though the former is shorter and more often used. The days when each is to be used are fixed. If we were to attend an Orthodox service we should find that people stand or kneel, or occasionally prostrate themselves, as they did in St Sophia; they never sit. In fact they move about anywhere in the nave, perhaps lighting a candle, or it may be saluting an icon. An icon is "a picture of a sacred subject painted upon a panel of wood" and is often covered with a casing of metal, which may be precious, and adorned with precious stones. Since the eighth century Orthodoxy has not allowed statues, but has held the icon in great veneration. The *iconostasis*, which cuts off the sanctuary (i.e. the part corresponding to what is beyond the altar rails in an English church, not the whole chancel) is covered with icons. Orthodox Christians have them also in their homes. In the Orthodox service the deacon plays a more important part than in the West. Most of the time he stands, facing the sanctuary, just outside the royal doors—the double doors in the middle of the *iconostasis*. His task is to lead the people in prayer—but there is little in which they can join audibly except the Lord's Prayer and the Creed. The deacon chants the Gospel from the pulpit; and it is accompanied by a great deal of ceremony, including a Gospel procession.

Another and even more elaborate procession comes at what is called the Great Entrance, i.e. the Offertory, the bringing in of the paten (with bread on it) and the chalice (with wine). For these portions of the service the royal doors are opened, as they are for the communion of the laity, for which the priest comes into the body of the church. Nowadays the priest at the altar (the Orthodox call it the throne) cannot be seen and can only occasionally be heard, as when he raises his voice at the consecration to say "Take, eat; this is my Body which is broken for you for the remission of sins", and, "Drink ye all of this; this is my Blood of the New Testament, which is shed for you and for many for the remission of sins . . . changing them (i.e. the bread and wine) by the Holy Spirit." When St Sophia was built, however, you would have heard the whole service, for Justinian insisted upon this; and you would have seen more. There would also have been more communicants, who received their communion in both kinds, the bread being placed in their hands. To-day only the officiant and the other clergy make their communion in both kinds separately, the laity being communicated in both kinds together by means of a spoon. The Orthodox never have more than one celebration on one day and every celebration is a high or sung celebration, with full ceremonial.[1]

DIFFERENCES OF RITE AND CUSTOM

"Strangers from Rome" and even some Englishmen found their way to Constantinople, either as merchants or as pilgrims or as members of the Emperor's foreign bodyguard. This was at first largely composed of Russians but later, by 1054, of Scandinavians and Englishmen. For these folk from the West there were churches in Constantinople which followed the Latin use, just as there were churches in Rome which followed the Greek or Orthodox use. (Part of southern Italy at this time belonged to the Byzantine Empire, and in 1024 Pope John XIX recognized the Byzantine ecclesiastical province of Bari, with its archbishop and twelve bishops who came under Constantinople.) Probably, if you had come from the West and were

[1] I. F. Hapgood: *The Service Book of the Holy Orthodox Catholic Apostolic Church*, New York, 1922, has been followed in this paragraph. According to G. Every, *The Byzantine Patriarchate*, p. 30, weekly communion was not unusual as late as the ninth century—long after the practice had ceased in the West.

living in Constantinople, you would have gone to the services that you were used to; but, if this had not been possible, you would soon have discovered that, despite superficial differences, the rites were fundamentally the same. The order was the same: an introductory part, whether it were the Mass or the Liturgy, included the Gospel; then came the sermon (if there was one); the offertory; the prayers leading to the consecration and communion; the brief concluding section. In 1053–4 the Greeks made a grievance of the fact that the Latins used unleavened bread while they used leavened: two hundred years before, the patriarch Photius, in his quarrel with Rome, had the same grievance. The difference of usage plainly went back for centuries, and nobody knew how long.

Then there was the use of the vernacular. Constantinople showed the greater readiness to allow the use of native languages in worship, and we are told that "all the tribes north and east of the Black Sea had their own versions of the liturgy of Constantinople."[1] Nevertheless Rome could sanction the use of the vernacular, as she does to-day in the case of the Uniates, eastern Churches, using eastern rites but in communion with Rome. Pope Hadrian II not only authorized the Slavonic Liturgy which the brothers Cyril and Methodius, missionaries from Constantinople, had introduced into Moravia about 863, but at the instance of the two brothers ordained some young men as priests who were to use the Slavonic rite in Moravia, and in 870 consecrated Methodius as the first Moravo-Pannonian archbishop. Cyril had died the previous year, when the two brothers were in Rome. They do in fact illustrate in a remarkable way both how Rome and Constantinople could work together (for they themselves were easterns, born in Salonica and sent out not by the Church of Rome but by the Church of Constantinople), and also how at any time friction could arise between the two Churches. Like Pope Hadrian, his successor John VIII sanctioned the use of the Slav Liturgy, nevertheless Methodius met with almost consistent opposition from the bishops and clergy who followed the Latin rite. So great was the opposition that the Slav Liturgy never took root in Moravia, with the result that to-day Christians in Czecho-Slovakia are mostly Roman Catholic. It took firm hold however in Bulgaria, after the baptism of King Boris, who ruled for some forty years before ending his days in a monastery. He was baptized at Constantinople in 864. A century later, when the faith spread

[1] Every, *op. cit.*, p. 123.

to the region of Kiev and Vladimir and his people were baptized in the Dnieper, the Slavonic Liturgy became what it has
remained ever since, the liturgy of the Russian Church. Christians in Russia and in Bulgaria are for the most part members of
the Orthodox Church. But just as in the days of which we have
been thinking all sorts of tribes had versions of the Orthodox
rite in their own languages, so to-day, although Greek for the
Greek-speaking peoples and Old Slavonic for the Orthodox in

From *The Church of our Fathers*

AN EXAMPLE OF RUSSIAN CHURCH ARCHITECTURE
(NOTE THE SPIRAL OR "ONION" DOMES)

Russia and the Balkans are the two principal languages, you
could hear the Orthodox Liturgy in Japanese and Chinese, in
Arabic and Finnish, in English and German, and in other
languages too.

SCHISM: THE POINTS IN DISPUTE

It was nothing new in the eleventh century for the Churches of
Rome and Constantinople to be in schism. Official relations had
been broken off many times, and sometimes the break had lasted
many years, but this had made little difference. It would even
appear that in 1053–4, when Michael Cerularius the Patriarch

of Constantinople brought matters to a head, the two Churches were already estranged; an old schism going back to 1009 never having been officially healed.[1] Yet Church life was going on much as usual, and, whatever the differences of custom, there can have been few people except the Patriarch who would not have been glad to see the old estrangement healed, and fewer who desired a rent which would eventually become permanent. Emphatically the Byzantine Emperor did not wish it, for the Normans who were just then menacing the papal estates were equally a menace to the Byzantine cities of southern Italy. Political expediency suggested that Pope and Eastern Emperor should be friends.

Yet this was the time that Michael Cerularius chose to close all the churches in Constantinople which followed the Latin rite, a thing which had never been done before, schism or no schism. The Greek rite and that only might now be used, and when the Latin clergy refused, he excommunicated them. He and his friends brought out the old grievances, concentrating however so largely on the minor differences, like that about the use of unleavened bread, that we may be sure the root cause of the trouble lay deeper in a clash of personalities and wills.

Photius, at the time of the schism of 867-9, listed once and for all the main points in dispute. Only one was doctrinal, the Western doctrine of the "double procession" of the Holy Spirit. In the Nicene Creed the clause "and the Son" (*Filioque*) had been added after "who proceedeth from the Father". The Creed as accepted at the Council of Chalcedon had not the clause, and the East has never inserted it. How early the theory of the double procession arose in the West is not certainly known, but St Augustine of Hippo taught it.[2] The insertion first got into the Creed in Spain, at Toledo in 589; then the Frankish Church adopted it, and in 809 the Emperor Charlemagne ordered its retention in Frankish territory in opposition to the Pope, Leo III—not that Leo did not believe in the double procession, for he expressly says he did. The Popes cannot be held responsible for initiating this particular point of discord. Pope John VIII, in a letter to Photius, said that he himself never

[1] For this view, as against the older one found in the *Camb. Med. Hist.*, vol. 4, see Every, *op. cit.*, ch. xiv, where authorities are cited.

[2] "When the Holy Spirit," he wrote, "is said to proceed from the Father, it is to be understood that He proceeds also from the Son. . . . The Son is begotten of the Father, and the Holy Spirit proceeds from the Father as His Source; and by the Father's gift, without any interval of time, proceeds in common from Both."

used the interpolated form in reciting the Nicene Creed. The Creed had not at this date got into the Mass at Rome. This did not occur until 1014 when it was the interpolated form which was used. It would seem that even at the time of Photius East and West might have arrived at a formula on which both could have agreed, by adding the words *per Filium* "through the Son" rather than "and the Son". But by the time that Leo IX was Pope and Michael Cerularius Patriarch this could hardly have been accomplished. For one thing, Rome was now reciting *Filioque* in its Creed. In fact, however, this western addition to the Creed, which over the centuries has been felt as a real difficulty by the East, hardly entered into the disputes of 1053–4.

The three minor points of discord can be mentioned without comment. They were: (i) the use, as we have seen, of unleavened bread in the Eucharist in the West; (ii) the Saturday fast, which the Latins kept but the Greeks did not; (iii) the marriage of priests, which the East allowed if before ordination, although no married priest might become a bishop.

CAUSES KEEPING THE CHURCHES APART

There were, nevertheless, circumstances and factors which combined to keep the two Churches apart. Apart from psychological differences between the speculative and more mystical East and the practical, matter-of-fact West, there was difference of language. The Latins as a rule knew no Greek and the Greeks no Latin. Quite literally they did not understand one another. Once Greek had been spoken all round the Mediterranean seaboard but when Latin began to oust Greek in the West, after about A.D. 200, it is remarkable in how short a time hardly anybody in Rome could speak Greek. In the East Latin continued to be used as an official language until the Moslem conquests. Then it was dropped and even the clergy did not learn it. Nothing could have suited the Arabs better; it helped to divide Christendom.

It was the Arab policy to isolate Constantinople. How far they could succeed depended upon their control of the sea routes. They were sufficiently a maritime power to lay siege to Constantinople for a whole year, from August 717 to August 718, and this was only one of many sieges. Towards the end of the ninth century the Moslem and Norse pirates had a stranglehold on the Mediterranean, which was virtually closed to peaceful shipping; but in the tenth century things improved. The Arabs lost their strongholds in Italy and southern France,

and in 961 Crete was taken from them. With the revival of the
Byzantine navy maritime commerce revived; between the West
and Jerusalem there was a new flow of pilgrims which had
previously declined to almost vanishing point since the Carolingian times when Charlemagne himself had visited Jerusalem
and established friendly relations with the Caliph Haroun
al-Rashid; and many pilgrims as well as merchants chose to
call in at Constantinople on their way to or from the East.
They were specially attracted to Constantinople by its great
collection of relics. We must not imagine that Rome and
Constantinople were completely cut off from each other; even
when the sea routes were closed or hazardous there were the
land routes round the top of the Adriatic, though even here
Bulgars, Slavs and Lombards might be as troublesome to travellers as were Moslem pirates. Many circumstances did, nevertheless, tend to keep the rival cities apart.

Constantinople as a Church owed its standing to being the
Church of the capital city, New Rome. It had no other claim.
Byzantines might discover in St Andrew an apostolic founder
for their see, but the claim was hardly serious. Rome had never
owed its pre-eminence primarily to civil status; so that it was
not an all-important matter that Milan or Ravenna should
come to have higher civil standing. To begin with, Rome's pre-
eminence was due to the fact that its Church's "founders and
builders", as St Irenaeus said, were the *two* Apostles, St Peter
and St Paul. Afterwards St Peter overshadowed St Paul and
beginning with Siricius in 385 we find the Popes basing their
claim to authority on the mystical presence of St Peter with or
in each successive occupant of the papal see. No Church, not
even Constantinople, disputed that Rome ranked first among
Churches, and the Council of Chalcedon gave her "formal precedence" over all other Churches, while declaring the see of
Constantinople second in rank and independent of the jurisdiction of the papacy. Rome, however, demanded more than a
precedence of honour; the Pope as St Peter's successor claimed
to possess an authority and jurisdiction in some sense, over all
other Churches. Innocent I in 417 went so far as to say that
Rome was "the source of the whole episcopate". Even in the
West these exalted views were not at once accepted, though
Western Christianity came before long to mean Roman
Christianity. The phrase occurs in a letter addressed to the
Church of North Africa, which had sent him the findings of
two African councils, not because it submitted to his judgement

(as Innocent claimed) but in order to secure the concurrence of the papacy in the matter of Pelagius which concerned Rome. The African Church at the time of St Augustine still believed then, as had St Cyprian long before, in co-operation between the Churches of Christendom rather than the subordination of all the rest to one of them.[1] Roman claims were unlikely to find much favour in Constantinople. In the eleventh century, with Constantinople extending its sphere of influence in the Balkans, in Russia and in lands to the East, and with a Patriarch as forceful as Michael Cerularius, there was, humanly speaking, bound to be a collision.

For although Leo IX had succeeded to a papacy spiritually and materially impoverished and faced with all sorts of difficulties, yet he believed strongly in the spiritual authority of the Roman see. Michael Cerularius, able, proud and overbearing, with the Emperor apparently afraid of him, was intent upon making the Byzantine Church more important than the State, and upon becoming master of both. So he closed the Latin churches and ordered the abbots and monks of the monasteries attached to them to follow the Greek rite. There were scenes of violence and the Patriarch's chancellor, Nicephorus, is said to have trodden under foot the Host consecrated according to the Latin usage, saying it was unleavened and worthless.

In the summer of 1053 the Normans took Leo prisoner at Civitate, though they later released him. But Leo was not the man even in his hour of temporal defeat to countenance such occurrences. He sent three legates, one of whom was Cardinal Humbert, to the Emperor Constantine IX, with the object not only of winning over the Emperor (in which they were successful), but also of securing the condemnation and deposition of Michael. Leo passed over the minor points at issue and took his stand firmly on the question of jurisdiction. In April 1054, however, Leo died and though the legates no longer had authority to act, act they did. The thunderbolt came as the Liturgy was about to begin in the church of St Sophia. The legates entered, addressed the congregation, complained of the conduct of Michael, and laid the bull of excommunication on the altar.

[1] St Augustine *never* said "Rome has spoken. The cause is settled." What he said, though something like it, bore a quite different meaning. Pelagius, a monk from Britain, who was possibly Irish, taught that man is not sinful by nature; he can be good if he chooses, without the grace of God. He was well known in Rome and had many followers. St Augustine believed that human nature (but for God's grace) is entirely corrupt.

The excommunication was pronounced against Michael and his friends; they went on to state that they found Constantinopolitans as a whole orthodox.

The result was what we should expect. Public opinion at once forced the Emperor to break with Rome and side with the Patriarch. A synod was held in St Sophia; the Roman bull was condemned and a few days later burned. So, historians always used to say, began the final rupture of the two Churches. To-day this is questioned. The situation had not really changed except that a new bitterness was added. It has always been difficult to account for the fact that so little notice was anywhere taken of the rupture at the time; Churches like Antioch, for instance, remained in communion with both. Nor was Michael's own triumph lasting: the new Emperor, Isaac Comnenus deposed Michael in 1059 and he died in exile. The Latin churches in Constantinople were at once re-opened. But the bitterness had sunk deep. Then came the Crusades. From the first the easterns resented the arrogance and what they thought to be the boorishness of the Crusaders, quite apart from their propensity to strife and pillage. But it is clear that the personal representative of Pope Urban II on the first Crusade, Bishop Adhemar of Le Puy (whose death after the taking of Antioch was a major tragedy) was ready and anxious to co-operate with Orthodox Christians, whom he showed no signs of regarding as not in communion with the West. It was the Crusaders' later actions in parcelling out the East into Latin kingdoms, and in particular in sacking Constantinople itself in 1204 amid scenes of indescribable horror, which finally separated the Churches. A Latin Patriarch was set up in St Sophia, and, though the Latin Patriarchate was short-lived, the two Churches never came together again. There were attempts at reunion, always occasioned by Constantinople's need of material help against the Turk. Rome's price was always the same. Even though emissaries from the East might be prepared to barter the independence of their Churches, as at the Council of Florence in 1439, on their return they would find their action repudiated. The hero in 1439 was Mark of Ephesus, the one delegate who had refused to yield; and the Russian Church was later to regard the fall of Constantinople to the Turks in 1453, fourteen years afterwards, as a punishment for coming to terms with the West in a vain quest for material aid which the Pope was powerless to supply.

A CHURCH IN BONDAGE

When a synod held in Constantinople in 1470 formally denounced the union promulgated at Florence, the Orthodox world with the exception of Russia and Crete had come under Turkish rule. The older Churches such as Antioch and Alexandria, had been under Moslem rule for many centuries even then. Russia had not long freed herself from Tartar rule, a rule which had borne more heavily on the Church after the acceptance of Islam by the Tartars than it had at first. From then on until modern times, the Russian Church was destined to be practically the only Orthodox Church not in bondage in a non-Christian State. And naturally this has had its effect. The Russian Church has had extensive missions, in fact wherever the Russian has gone he has taken his Church—into Siberia, to Japan (where there were forty thousand Orthodox Christians in 1931), and by way of the Aleutian Islands and Alaska into North America. But for most of the Orthodox Churches such activity was ruled out. Christians might practise their religion but not parade it.

"Orthodoxy lived for centuries under the harsh government of the Turk. But with the coming of political emancipation, it is found to have retained its faith intact, its identity unimpaired and its unity preserved. It has known how to bend before the storm and, unbroken, to abide its time. Doubtless it has had its sinners, its time-servers even in high places. But the twofold cry of Orthodoxy, 'Lord, have mercy' and 'Glory be to Thee, O Lord', has rung out above them all and still rings out. The host of its saints and prelates and of common folk held fast to their faith in the power of the Resurrection to transform the whole world, and they have seen and see in Orthodoxy the authentic faith of Christ, for which many of them have been prepared to die."[1]

Though St Sophia became a mosque and then, when Turkey became a secular State after the first World War, a science museum, Constantinople has nevertheless remained the chief of the eastern patriarchates.

[1] R. M. French: *The Eastern Orthodox Church*, p. 173.

15

The Papal Monarchy

Our concern in this chapter is with three questions which are immensely important if we are to understand the history of Western Christendom. They are: How did the medieval conception of the Papacy arise? What did it imply? When did the papacy reach the climax of its power?

ST AUGUSTINE OF HIPPO AND THE "CITY OF GOD"

In order to answer these questions it will be best to begin by going back all the way to St Augustine, who was from 396 to 430 Bishop of Hippo, then the next important town to Carthage on the coast of North Africa. It is not too much to say that St Augustine of Hippo has influenced Western Christianity more than anyone else except St Paul. One of the ways will appear in this chapter.

He was born at Thagaste in North Africa, his father being a pagan, his mother the pious and gentle Monica. Perhaps it was through her prayers that her son at last became a Christian, when he was thirty-two. St Augustine tells us in his *Confessions* how, just before she died, they talked together of the Kingdom of Heaven as they leaned on the ledge of a window looking down on the garden of their house at Ostia, at the mouth of the Tiber. They were on their way home to Africa from Italy, not long after Augustine's baptism. The most famous sentence in the *Confessions* everyone ought to know—"Thou hast made us for Thyself, and restless is my heart until it comes to rest in Thee" (*Fecisti enim nos ad te, et cor inquietum donec requiescat in te*).

While Augustine was Bishop of Hippo Rome fell to Alaric the Goth in 410. This was an event which shook the world. No hostile army had entered Rome for eight hundred years, People asked, as they were bound to do, why Rome had fallen. and the heathen blamed Christianity. They said that when Rome had honoured the old gods she had prospered. It was to meet this challenge that Augustine wrote *The City of God* (*De Civitate Dei*). It is a very long work, in twenty-two books, and it took

110

thirteen years to complete, but in it Augustine showed that it was the virtues of the old Rome, not the worship of the old gods (who had not saved other cities from disaster) that had made her great. Not till half-way through did he reach his great theme, the two kingdoms or cities, the *Civitas Dei* and the *civitas terrena*, the City of God and the earthly city, the latter identified with the Roman Empire. For the time being, he said, the two were all mixed up together; but the final portion of the one would be "the peace of God", of the other, punishment.

THE TWO POWERS

What is the City of God? No more can fairly be said than that Augustine tended to identify it with the visible Catholic Church on earth. But, whether the City be the Church or, in a wider sense, Christendom, the Christian world, he was not, in his book, concerned with the question as to exactly who should govern it. St Augustine comes into the picture because it was he who was responsible for the idea of the two cities, not because he would necessarily have approved of what later generations made of it. Even when Rome fell it would have been possible to speak of Roman Christendom, for the barbarians who took it were themselves Christians of sorts, and before so very long most of Europe was to come under Christian rule. When, some sixty years after Augustine's death, Pope Gelasius I (492–6) dealt for the first time with the question of government, he did so with Christian countries in mind. He said there were two powers —bishops and kings—governing the world, and he put bishops first. Further, God had caused the bishop of Rome "to be preferred above all bishops." Indeed, the Popes had for some time claimed—ever since Siricius in 385, as we saw in the last chapter —not merely to be the successors of St Peter but to possess the authority of St Peter mystically present in them.

It was commonly held that "the powers that be", the secular powers, were "ordained of God" (Rom. 13. 1). Gelasius's opinion need mean no more than that they are subject to the spiritual power in matters where the salvation of souls is at stake. This was, many years later, to be the view of St Thomas Aquinas (1226).[1] But it could imply a great deal more, and before the time of Aquinas the Papacy had come in practice to set its authority much higher. The conception of the two powers reflects, however, the relation of Church and State through the

[1] See Jalland: *The Church and the Papacy*, pp. 410, 411.

Dark Ages (500–800) and the Middle Ages. Of the two almost everybody believed that the State was supreme right up to about the time of our own Norman Conquest. The Church's task was to make rulers and their subjects Christians and better Christians. Rulers, for their part, believed that they had the right, and indeed a positive duty, to intervene in religious matters. They simply would not have understood if anyone had said that this implied hostility to Rome. Bishops and kings were there to co-operate in a common task, the establishment of a Rule of Christ on earth. (It was a magnificent ideal, if never more than very partially realized because of course men were not equal to the conception.) But if bishops and kings should come into conflict, supremacy lay with the monarch not the bishop, the Emperor not the Pope.

THE CAROLINGIAN AND THE HOLY ROMAN EMPIRE

Never was a more masterful monarch than Charlemagne, to all intents Emperor of the West long before Pope Leo III crowned him in St Peter's on Christmas Day, 800, when the people shouted "Hail to Charles the Augustus, crowned of God, the great and peace-bringing Emperor of the Romans." Charles acquiesced but was not too pleased. Why? It might have been thought that he owed his right to rule to the Church, and this he did not believe. After his death in 814, his son Louis the Pious crowned himself, taking the crown from the altar in St Peter's as a gift from God, his father and the nation. Charles was a Frank, with his capital at Aachen, and he ruled over Europe from the Elbe to the Ebro. In Italy he gave lands taken from the Lombards to the Pope, as his father Pepin the Short had done before him. These Papal States, which came later on to stretch diagonally across Italy, made the Pope an independent temporal ruler, who had his own army like any other temporal ruler.

But these developments lay in the future. Charles was the patron and protector of the Holy See. A mosaic in the Lateran shows him kneeling with Pope Leo III before St Peter. The wording reads: "Holy Peter, thou bestowest life on Pope Leo and victory on King Charles." Charles felt called of God to take the helm of both Church and State throughout his dominions. So he interpreted *The City of God*, which he used to have read to him at meals. He controlled Church property with papal approval, and appointed to Church offices, and made laws covering every side of life. One made death the penalty for not fasting in Lent! Another law imposed the tithe (a tenth of one's substance or labour) on all alike, nobles, free men and serfs. His most attractive side is as the patron of learning; his palace school, where scholars and nobles, laymen and ecclesiastics met and whose master was an Englishman, Alcuin of York, set on foot a revival of letters. Popes, if they differed from him, usually came round to his views, which he never doubted were right. But there was only one Charlemagne. On the death of Louis the Pious (840), the Carolingian Empire split into three.

From *The Church of our Fathers*

HEAD OF CHARLEMAGNE

In less than twenty years, and less than half a century after Charles's death, it was the Pope, Nicholas I (858–67), who was strong, not any secular ruler. When he said "that which the Pope has decided is to be observed by all", they were no idle words. "The real creator of the Papacy, as we know it in the next six centuries, was ... Nicholas I".[1] Bishops and archbishops might be supported by Carolingian princes but both they and the princes were brought to heel. Papal control over the Church tightened. For an archbishop to act as metropolitan of a province he must have received the *pallium* at the Pope's hands. This was a Y-shaped piece of stuff, rather like a stole, made of white wool and worn on the shoulders, falling

[1] Jalland: *The Church and the Papacy*, p. 378.

singly in front and behind. Under Nicholas, too, we see developing a universal Church law—the canon law.[1] Nicholas accepted the collection known as the *Forged Decretals*. The title is not very exact, for much of the collection consists of genuine Church laws, but, though Nicholas probably did not know it, forged matter was included. The aim of whoever made the compilation (probably in France, *c.* 850) was to protect the ordinary bishop from lay or episcopal interference by asserting again and again the right of appeal to the Pope, the successor of St. Peter. Appeal to the Pope, from being a rare thing, was thus on the way to becoming the regular thing, which would, of course immeasurably strengthen the papal position.

In 962 the German king, Otto I, revived the imperial title and the Holy Roman Empire was born; it claimed to continue the Carolingian Empire. Its rulers were the Popes' opposite numbers all through the Middle Ages. But not for many years was there another Pope of Nicholas's stature. The two powers remained, each supreme in its own sphere, on the whole working together in friendly co-operation or rivalry. Never were relations better than in A.D. 1000. Then the papacy passed through one of its very worst periods. Some of the Popes elected (the Roman nobility swaying the elections) were quite unfit to rule. In 1046 the Emperor Henry III performed a signal service when he set aside three rival Popes and chose a German bishop to occupy and restore moral authority to the see of St Peter. A few years later Leo IX (who, as we saw in the last chapter, asserted papal authority over Constantinople as Nicholas had done before him) was also Henry's nominee. Leo never spared himself in the work of reform, crossing and recrossing the Alps to restore Rome's lost moral ascendancy.

HILDEBRAND (GREGORY VII)

In 1059 a synod held at the Lateran[2] decreed that for the future Popes were to be elected by the cardinal bishops, with no lay interference; the Church was going to be master in its own house. In 1073 Hildebrand was elected Pope. His twelve years' reign altered the whole relation between Church and State. We should notice that William I was king of England during his

---

[1] The word canon = "a straight rod" or "rule" for measuring; so the canons offered a rule of right conduct.

[2] i.e. the church of St John Lateran, in Rome, scene of many famous councils in the Middle Ages.

entire pontificate (1073–85). To a certain extent they came into collision. But if William flatly refused to acknowledge Gregory as his temporal overlord, he never questioned his spiritual primacy, and the Pope did not press his claims. By the standards of the day William was a good churchman. "The Conqueror's wrath vented itself in slaughter, and he loved money as he loved the tall deer, but he could be true to a high standard; he heard Mass daily, he was unswervingly loyal to wife and councillors."[1] He made Church appointments but he made good ones, as when he brought Lanfranc from Bec to be archbishop of Canterbury. William let him go to Rome to get his *pallium*, but not when Gregory summoned him several times afterwards. Lanfranc, when the Pope censured him for not obeying, did not reply. When he had been abbot of Bec, Popes had not issued orders to archbishops. In this respect the canon law, which Lanfranc knew well, for he brought a collection to England, had become a dead letter, and he was old-fashioned enough to believe that the metropolitan should be supreme in his own province. But Gregory VII intended *his* supremacy to cover every field.

His aims were twofold: (1) to reform the Church by means of the papal supremacy; (2) to liberate the Church from lay control.

He forbade lay investiture, i.e. the gift of ring and staff by a lay ruler to a bishop or abbot. Ring and staff were symbols of spiritual authority. There was a long struggle. The question was settled first in the case of England (1107). Bishops were to be chosen by the cathedral chapters in the king's presence; the bishop-elect was to do homage for his temporalities, but the archbishop would invest him with ring and staff after consecration. In the case of the Empire the settlement (1122) was very similar. The long struggle opened dramatically. The Emperor Henry IV had been high-handed in church matters, had invested a new archbishop of Milan, and had denounced Hildebrand as "not Pope, but false monk". The Pope replied by excommunicating Henry, releasing all men from their oaths to him and forbidding any to serve him. It was soon evident that the Pope would be obeyed. So in December Henry, with his wife and children, set out to cross the Alps. He found Gregory at Canossa and there for three days he waited barefoot in the snow in the courtyard as a suppliant. On January 28th Gregory

---

[1] K. Feiling: *A History of England*, p. 113.

absolved him, receiving his crown into his hands. Henry received it back when he had sworn obedience to the papal will.

The Emperor, however, did not keep his promise and this time he was supported by others, including the German bishops, who said they "disliked being ordered about like bailiffs". There was civil war and Gregory died in exile, pronouncing his own epitaph: "I have loved righteousness and hated iniquity: therefore, I die in exile." It was true that he had a passion for *justitia*, "righteousness". He believed the papacy to be the source of all ecclesiastical authority, and he had found the secular powers to be the biggest obstacle to making *justitia* a living reality.

INNOCENT III

The papacy reached the summit of its influence when Innocent III was Pope (1198–1216). It is true to say that the papacy had become popular. Ecclesiastics and laymen alike had come to welcome papal control. There were two reasons for this. One was the canon law, which had become the law of the whole western Church: this made very prominent the obedience due to Rome, and bishops and others were genuinely impressed. Another reason was that lay rulers so often misused their powers. In England, while William I had used his powers over the Church with a sense of responsibility, William II left sees and abbeys vacant for his own and the treasury's gain. There were eleven abbeys vacant when he died. Anselm, Lanfranc's successor, believing that to disobey the Pope was to disobey St Peter and therefore to disobey God, was bound to fight for the Church's freedom from royal interference and for the right of appeal to Rome. All the English bishops had been with the Conqueror against Hildebrand, but some supported Anselm against Rufus. And the papal party grew. When Henry II quarrelled with Thomas Becket over the right of the Church to try and to sentence its own clerks accused of crimes, in its own courts, and in fact be supreme in its own house, the country was with Becket (and the Pope) and not the king. So also it was with Innocent III in his quarrel with King John. The England of John's day cannot have liked having its churches shut, sacraments forbidden to all except the dying, and the dead refused Christian burial—and this is what an interdict meant.[1] Yet, although Innocent placed England under an interdict in

---

[1] Mass might be heard once a week, but only outside the church.

1208, which lasted for five years, the country did not rally to the king. It was removed only when John admitted Stephen Langton as archbishop, and surrendered his crown to the Pope, receiving the country back as a papal vassal. Already Sicily, Portugal and Aragon were papal fiefs.

The papacy was attaining powers that could very easily be abused. When they were—as they soon were—the papal hold on Europe lessened. But what we have seen in the case of England was true of Europe as a whole in the earlier half of the thirteenth century. The liberty which the Church desired was not liberty from papal interference but from royal interference; or, as Professor Z. N. Brooke has expressed it, "liberty to be under papal control."[1] The evil days of "provision", by which the Pope arbitrarily presented foreign ecclesiastics to benefices, and thrust foreign nominees into bishoprics, had barely begun.[2]

[1] *The English Church and the Papacy from the Conquest to the Reign of John*, p. 17.
[2] For "provision" and its effects in England, see ch. 19.

16

Church Life in the Middle Ages

Up and down the country the great Norman churches are familiar landmarks. We know them by their great square towers, their semi-circular arches, their stone roofs, their massive round columns (which, however, were filled with rubble), their zig-zag ornamentation and cushion capitals. No Saxon cathedral remains but the Norman buildings which replaced them do. Lanfranc at Canterbury set the example, rebuilding the cathedral in seven years on the model of the abbey church at Caen, but already by the time of St Anselm, his successor, it needed enlarging. That is typical. All through the Middle Ages these great churches were constantly being added to or altered, so that we nearly always find a mixture of styles. Norman architecture merged into Early English (known by the pointed arch), Early English into Decorated (known by its elaborately traceried windows), and then, about 1350, followed the Perpendicular style with its vertical lines.

But a medieval church is most inadequately described if we think only in terms of architecture. What did these great churches in fact mean to those who built them and worshipped in them? "Cathedral and monastic churches alike were founded for the same general object," says Professor A. Hamilton Thompson, "the perpetual celebration of divine worship by a body of men set apart for that purpose." In a monastic church, such as the cathedrals at Canterbury and Winchester and Durham, they would be monks; in a non-monastic cathedral, such as St Paul's or Salisbury or York, they would be canons, who contrary to the monks, might sometimes employ deputies. But we must not think of the worship as being offered simply and solely to the glory of God: its intention was also to benefit the living and the dead. People in the Middle Ages never for long forgot the dead, or their own death one day. The walls of both parish churches and cathedrals were bright with paintings, and prominent among them would be the Day of Doom. At Lutterworth church the Doom, which must have been a familiar

118

sight to Wiclif in the fourteenth century, may still be seen; and there is a particularly fine example over the chancel-arch in St Thomas's church, Salisbury. In the great cathedral and abbey churches intercession for the dead never relaxed. Yet if the living could help the dead by their prayers, so could the saints help the living, for men in the Middle Ages thought of the saint —particularly a saint whose body lay in their own church, or a saint of whom they possessed some relic, as a living power actively sharing their interests and affairs, able to help, or to hinder, should they be angered. That is why pilgrims flocked to the great pilgrimage churches; to Canterbury, "the holy blisful martir for to seke", or to such older shrines as those of St Swithun at Winchester, St Edmund at Bury St Edmunds, and St Cuthbert at Durham.

Canterbury, of course, had other saints besides St Thomas Becket. There were, in addition to Becket's shrine, which towered above the high altar, the shrines of St Dunstan and St Alphege, on the right and left of it. St Anselm, too, lay in his church. And if St Augustine (like Theodore of Tarsus and other early archbishops) lay in a splendid shrine in his monastery outside the city walls, he was still a Canterbury saint. All would have more than one special day when high festival would be kept. So we find St Thomas commemorated on the day of his martyrdom (December 29th), on the day of his return from exile (December 2nd), and on the day of his translation (July 7th). As the late Dr C. S. Phillips remarks in that quarry of interesting information, *Canterbury Cathedral in the Middle Ages*, it must have been quite a problem getting all the special days in.

MONASTERY

The great Benedictine houses were in, or close to, large centres of population. Many of the English cathedrals were Benedictine houses. It was the Cistercians, a late order (their first house in England being Waverley Abbey, 1129) who chose the wildest spots in which to settle—Yorkshire dales or Welsh valleys or Hampshire marsh-lands. It was the Cistercians who gave their houses such lovely names as Waverley, Fountains, Grace Dieu, Valle Crucis, Beaulieu, Rievaulx. They employed lay brothers called *conversi* to till the soil or raise the sheep. These were quite illiterate; they learnt to say a few prayers by heart, heard Mass on Sundays and very occasionally in the week, and received communion seven times in the year. In a Cistercian house they might outnumber the choir monks by three to one. In the older Benedictine monasteries (there were fifty-seven independent Benedictine houses in England and Wales by 1300) most monks were in priests' orders. Some however were in minor orders, and there might be a few boys (the monks of the future), though it became less and less common to train boys in the monasteries. Treble voices for the choir, if they were wanted for High Mass, might be imported from what we should call a choir school outside the monastery walls. In the Benedictine monastery you would find, in addition to the monks, not lay brothers but hired servants, who were there to do the manual work that the monks once did for themselves. There were also guests and lodgers. These last might be men or women, who had given lands or money in exchange for permanent board and lodging for themselves and their families. The families might include children, who would grow up in monastic surroundings but would not necessarily become monks or nuns themselves. There were many fewer nunneries but the same thing happened there, and the nuns in particular took boy and girl boarders.

THE "OPUS DEI"

The primary purpose of every monastery, as of every cathedral, was the worship of God. Worship was the Work of God (*opus Dei*) for which the monk was separated from the world. His monastery might be set in the midst of a city with many churches; Winchester, never a big city, had about twenty, Norwich over fifty; but the monk never took any of the services in them. Not that there was any need that he should, for these little city parishes, of about two hundred population, were more than adequately staffed. What, however, of the daily round in the monastic church itself?

It began at midnight (at least on Sundays, when the services were longer, on other days perhaps not till two a.m.) with the singing of Mattins (cf. "O Lord our heavenly Father . . . who hast safely brought us to the *beginning* of this day . . ."). The monks would rise from their beds in the dorter, and wearing their thick black woollen habits, with fur caps on their heads in winter, proceeded two by two down the night stair into the dimly lit church. Bowls filled with tallow were used for illumination, with here and there a candle, but the monks would not need lights in their stalls. They knew the services by heart. The first thing a novice had to do was to learn the Latin Psalter, and he would never have a chance of forgetting it. Immediately after Mattins came another shorter office called Lauds (our Mattins combines the two); then he could return to bed till daybreak. Since you went to bed at or soon after dark, your days in summer would be much longer than in winter and you would be glad of supper as well as dinner, which was your only winter meal. By the thirteenth century meat was eaten, except by the young monks, and except in Lent. From daybreak onwards you would be constantly in church. Including Mattins and Lauds there were eight offices, all of them sung, besides the daily High Mass which all the community attended. This would probably be about ten o'clock, and before it on Sundays and festivals there would be a procession, when the various shrines and sacred spots would be visited. There would be a shorter procession at Vespers. Sometimes for these a whole monastery would wear copes: Canterbury at the Dissolution possessed two hundred and sixty-two. The day would end with Compline. As for the singing, plain-chant was used, often unaccompanied; but organs were in use, usually little ones—Winchester possessed a huge organ of four hundred pipes which was said to take seventy men to blow! Two monks played it, and, as the monk Wulfstan said, "So swell[ed] the sound that . . . you must clap your hands to your ears."

Whatever else a monk did, whether it were copying or illuminating manuscripts, teaching novices, or working in the garden, though manual work was left more and more to others, the daily round of offices and masses (including individual masses, said for the living and the dead, at many side altars) was what supremely mattered. Nevertheless the business side of the monastery had to be carried on, and those monks so occupied were excused attending many of the services, or came in for part only.

MANOR

A monastery was divided into departments, each under its own head called an *obedientiary*. The Cellarer, who was really the caterer, visited markets and fairs to buy produce. The Guest-Master received all visitors. The Chamberlain looked after the linen, the Master of the Works the fabric, the Librarian the manuscripts, the Infirmarian the sick. Each had his own income, drawn from rents, from church livings appropriated to the monastery, or from manors. Lands formerly given to the monastery were subsequently allocated to some particular office. Thus at St Swithun's, the cathedral monastery at Winchester, three-quarters of the Almoner's income came from the manor at Hentone, eight miles east of the city across the downs, and which according to Domesday Book "was always the minster's". In the sixteenth century Hentone came to be called Hinton Amner or Ampner, because it had once belonged to the Almoner.

How did the Almoner employ his income? What did he do? Originally his main duty was to watch over the sick and helpless outside the monastery walls, and to feed the needy traveller. But as time went on the Almonry funds came to be used rather differently. Sometimes they went to support a school. At Norwich the Almoner supported the Grammar School; at Canterbury, too, the Almonry provided a school for poor children. If you had lived in a town you would very likely have had a chance of schooling, but not if you lived in the country, unless a kindly parish priest were able and willing to teach you. At Winchester the Almoner supported not a school but a small Sisters' Hospital just outside the monastery walls. There were about twenty sisters and they had their own chaplain who at first lived in a little house adjoining and in later days lodged in the monastery. He was, of course, a secular priest like the parish clergy, not a monk, and the Almoner paid him 13s. 4d. a year. (It is misleading to try to give equivalent money values; all one can really say is that money was worth very much more then than now. But even multiplying by seventy, which is one estimate, 13s. 4d. a year was little.) Roughly half the income of the Almonry was spent on this Sisters' Hospital. But the Almoner also paid for large quantities of bread to be given to the poor six times a year; and for expenses at Hinton, including "courtesies" (gifts) to the Prior's household there, perhaps at Christmas. Then there were "courtesies" to the Prior—St Swithun's being a cathedral monastery its head was a prior, not an abbot—and others every September on the occasion of St Giles's Fair.

This was the greatest fair of southern England and one of the five great fairs of northern Europe, to which foreign traders came from France, the Netherlands, the Rhineland, Italy and Spain. The Irish were always there, and as for London, all legal business ceased during the sixteen days that the fair lasted, which, as Mr Brian Vesey-Fitzgerald says, "is about the best indication you could have of the importance of the occasion."

But apart from the voluntary closing down of legal business in London, in Winchester itself and for miles around all buying and selling had to cease except at the fair; even the keys of the city's gates had to be handed over by the mayor and bailiffs to the Bishop of Winchester's seneschal. It was a bishop's fair and the Church took all the profits. Good Catholic townsfolk were often in the Middle Ages bitterly anti-clerical. This may help to explain why. One year for instance the citizens of Southampton, just outside the circuit of the bishop's authority, decided to be awkward and many of the foreign merchants never got to the fair at all.[1]

A monastic manor, like one belonging to a lay lord, had its free men and its villeins, who were tied to the soil and compelled to work for their lord on certain days every week, and whose daughters could not marry without their lord's consent. No doubt in a good year both monastery and local inhabitants prospered, and in a bad year both suffered. In 1352 there were no apples on the Hinton estate; therefore there was no cider at the monastery, and presumably the rector's household went without its Christmas present of a pipe of cider. This was three years after the Black Death and its effects were still being felt. (At Hinton there was a new rector in the year of the Black Death, but whether because his predecessor had been a victim or not we do not know.) Three years later there were only six inmates in the hospital including brothers as well as sisters; and there was nothing with which to buy them new clothing. Nor did the chaplain get his fee that year. But cloth, bread and silver were distributed to the poor, to the value of 5s. 6d., and the Prior got his usual "courtesy". When on April 14th, 1405, a fire destroyed the manor farm-house, and corn, horses, oxen and five carts with all their gear were lost, again the sisters got no new clothing, and this time the Hinton steward received no fee. Perhaps the fire was held to be his fault! The farm-house was not immediately rebuilt and no doubt the estate ceased to be a favourite spot for the monks to ride out to for brief visits or longer holidays. (It is a curious thought that they were among the very few people who did have holidays then.) The expenses of monks *in vices* (on visits) are recorded again and again. A reeve looked after the Hinton estate. He would live at the manor farm-house, and there the monks would stay, saying their offices in the oratory.

[1] For a description, see Mr B. Vesey-Fitzgerald's *Winchester*, ch. 9.

PARISH

It is unlikely that they joined in the worship of the parish church. But here at Hinton in the parish church those who lived and worked on the estate would meet week by week at least, every Sunday for Mass, paying the rector his customary dues four times in the year—at Christmas and Easter, on All Saints' Day (the local saint's day) and at the Dedication (the date and day unfortunately now lost). And in the parish church every day the rector or a curate would say Mass, served by the parish clerk, who with the curate and the page (a boy kept to do the housework) made up the rector's *familia* (family). There might even have been two curates. The rectory itself, if it were like most rectories of those days, would only have been a rough cottage, probably built of timber and very much like those the peasants lived in. Occasionally a parsonage-house would be better-built. There would be one bedroom for the residents— the two or three clergymen, the clerk and the boy, and one bedroom kept for guests; a small hall and a kitchen, with a bakehouse and a brewery. All was very cramped, with not much furniture and not many books, for books cost a lot of money. Nor was there time to study much, with so much needing to be done on the farm, not to mention visiting the sick, saying the offices and the other duties of a clergyman's life. Outside the rectory would be the farm-yard and the farm buildings—the tithe-barn, for the tithe was paid in kind, the cow-sheds, the pig-styes and stabling for the horses. One year, of the two hundred and twenty-six lambs which were born, twenty were paid to the rector as tithe, and, in the same year, of four calves we learn that one was eaten on the estate, one sent as a gift to the Prior, one sold, and one paid in tithe. Another year the Almoner makes a note, of which we do not know the outcome, about the rector "clamouring to have his pigs"!

In the thirteenth century there was much church-building going on. Hinton was only one of many places which largely rebuilt their Saxon churches. We can imagine a rector of those days, towards the end of the century, crossing his farm-yard, climbing the last little bit of the hill to the church, entering the recently rebuilt church by the priest's door in the south wall of the chancel, still remaining to this day and, unless the clerk had done this already, taking the sacred vessels from the small cupboard at the back of the double *piscina*, and preparing them on the shelf above. (Both shelf and piscina are still in use.)

He would take his vestments from the box in which they were
kept, and would vest in the chancel. Churches in those days
possessed no vestries. Nor would the church have possessed
many books; there would be just the service books which the
officiant and the clerk needed; perhaps there was not even a
complete Latin Bible, for complete Bibles were very expensive;
all that was in fact required would be those parts which were read
in the services. Perhaps on the altar would be one single candle,
a common usage in the later Middle Ages, or at the most two;
often there were none. The pre-Reformation Church was not
fussy about these things.[1]

Let us suppose that mass is over, and to-day, instead of going
straight back to his pigs or his ploughing, the rector is taking
the Blessed Sacrament (Reserved) to someone who is sick. He
would wear his surplice, and the clerk would go in front,
carrying the cross and a lantern and ringing the "tintinnabulum".
The whole usually received communion only once a year, at
Easter, but the sick were communicated weekly. Perhaps, when
the rector got back to the church, there would be a newly born
infant to baptize, for children were brought on the day of their
birth for baptism. In those days everybody thought, with
Langland, that "A bairn without baptism may not be saved".
Water was kept always ready in a locked font. Perhaps, instead
of a baby awaiting baptism, there would be children to be
presented for confirmation. Bishops when they were passing
near a parish would warn the clergy to bring the children to be
confirmed, sometimes confirming them in the open but often in
the parish church. So on his way from Winchester to his estate
at Meon the bishop might turn off the road and ride up the hill
to Hinton church to confirm half a dozen little boys and girls,
much too young to have any sort of preparation. But what teaching the clergy of those days gave would have been to the children; though some bishops urged their clergy to preach, and, in
their sermons, to give good advice about all sorts of matters.
One bishop of Durham told his clergy to announce every
Sunday that children must not be left alone in a house with a
fire or close to water.

Whatever other impressions one gets, there is the impression
of a Church which was part and parcel of the everyday life of
town and village. When a village held festivities, it was not

[1] Cf. Dix: *The Shape of the Liturgy*, pp. 419 sq. P. Dearmer: *The Parson's Handbook*, has plates showing medieval altars with a single light.

thought irreverent that they should be held in the churchyard, or even in the church itself.[1]

[1] The information about Hinton Ampner given in this chapter is taken from the *Compotus Rolls of the Obedientiaries of St Swithun's Priory, Winchester* (ed. Kitchen, Hampshire Record Society). The Almoner's Rolls are the best preserved of all the Rolls.

17

Monks, Friars and Crusaders

THE MONASTERY WALL

The Close wall at Winchester follows the line of the one which St Swithun had built to protect the minster from the Danes and which later enclosed the monastic buildings of St Swithun's Priory. Mr Brian Vesey-Fitzgerald tells us that he has found growing on this wall all the wild plants which you would expect to find and one or two that, in England, you would not. He goes on: "It is very difficult now, when walking through the Close, to realize that up to at least the dissolution of the monasteries, it was quite different in appearance. The lawns and the trees look so ancient and loved and tended that it is hard to believe that there was once, in all probability, only one lawn within the Close Wall and that would have been in the Cloister Garth. All the rest would have been buildings." [1]

The wall remains, still in places eighteen feet high, but of course "repaired and patched many many times in the course of the centuries"—the great monastic wall which symbolized and up to a point effected the monks' separation from the world. Here within the monastery—it might be at Winchester or Glastonbury, at Peterborough or Ely, at Canterbury or Bury St Edmunds—they served God and saved their souls. Theirs was a spiritual family whose life and work began and ended in the family circle.[2] It had not always been so, for monks had been great missionaries and sometimes great prophets of righteousness. But in the thirteenth century there was little missionary fervour within the walls of the monastery. The monks stood apart from the life going on around them, except when they made it serve their own purposes. Thus the possession of lands meant intercourse with the world, but through holidays for the monks themselves, and not through their ministering to those who lived and worked on the estates. The parish priest, indeed, might well have resented it had they tried. But all this goes to

[1] Cf. B. Vesey-Fitzgerald: *Winchester*, pp. 93–95.
[2] Cf. Dom David Knowles: *The Monastic Order in England*, p. 4.

127

show just how separate the monastic orders were. They were also aristocratic. By the thirteenth century most monks were drawn from the upper classes.

HOW FRIARS DIFFERED FROM MONKS

This was never so with the friars. Their leaders might come, like St Francis, of merchant stock, or belong to the nobility, but for the most part the friars came of the people. But what is more important, their aim was not to serve God by separating themselves from the world but rather the reverse. The friar, like the monk, was under a three-fold vow of poverty, chastity and obedience, but he sought to serve God by mixing with the world and carrying the Gospel to the world. So we look for the friary in the poorest district of a town, where the slum dwellers were certainly not the monks' concern and were too often neglected by the parish clergy. The friary itself would be a humble dwelling with walls of mud rather than of stone. And whereas the monastic church was the pride of every monk and the centre of his life, the friars might be years before they built a church of their own in the places where they ministered. So we find them working in Cambridge eight years before they built a church there, and in London fifteen years. They would worship at the parish church, for their relations with the parish clergy were better than with the monastic orders, who resented them. When we hear of the "great difficulties" which the friars had to face at Winchester, it is "an almost certain reference to monastic interference".[1] When the friars did build churches—and this is especially true of the Dominicans, the great preaching order— they built them with large, open naves as little obstructed by pillars as possible, obviously so that the congregation could see the preacher. The Franciscans felt less need of churches of their own and were very slow in building them. They had, however, an intense reverence for the Blessed Sacrament; and it was they who introduced the Christmas Crib.

GREY FRIARS AND BLACK FRIARS

The story of St Francis is so well known that little need be said about him. He was born at Assisi in Tuscany in 1182; he died in 1226. He was twenty-four when he left his father's house for good and wedded the Lady Poverty. He clad himself in a rough

[1] J. R. H. Moorman: *Church Life in England in the Thirteenth Century*, p. 376. There is a useful chapter on the friars.

"Picture Post"

THE CRUSADES.   SIEGE BY CATAPULTS

Illustration by Gustave Doré from "Histoire des Croisades" by
J. F. Michaud (1875).   (See pages 108, 132–5)

Paul Popper, Ltd.

THE CRUSADES.   ALEPPO SHOWING THE OLD WALLS BUILT BY THE CRUSADERS
(See pages 132–5)

"Picture Post"

JOHN WICLIF, A REFORMER BEFORE THE REFORMATION (1320–84)
(See page 148)

"Picture Post"

THE NEW LEARNING IN ENGLAND

Erasmus and Sir Thomas More visiting the children of Henry VII at
Greenwich, 1499.   (From the picture by J. Cadogan Cooper)

brown tunic which some peasant had given him and which meant, as G. K. Chesterton has said, that it was probably very old indeed, and had a piece of rope picked up at random for a girdle. That was in 1206. After three years two others joined him, Bernard of Quintavalle, a rich merchant of Assisi, and Peter, a canon of the cathedral, and 1209 is considered the date of the foundation of the order. Soon others joined them, and that year Francis and eleven companions visited Rome and got from the great Pope, Innocent III, his verbal confirmation of their rule of absolute poverty and devotion to good works. They were to be called *fratres minores*, Friars Minor, wear a dark grey habit and go barefoot. *Minores* were the poor as *majores* were the rich, so the name meant the Poor Brothers. The fixed rule was not drawn up till 1223, when Pope Honorius III confirmed it. The order grew rapidly and quickly spread throughout Europe and beyond.

Dominic de Guzman (1170–1221), the founder of the Dominicans, was a Spaniard, the son of a Castilian noble. Even before becoming, as a young man, a canon of the cathedral at Osma near his home, he was a noted preacher. When the bishop of Osma went to Provence on a mission connected with a contemplated royal marriage, he took Dominic with him as his chaplain, and in Provence he came into touch with heresy, which had come in from the East and had perilous consequences in the moral life of those who embraced it. At the root was the idea that spirit is good and matter evil. The same god did not make both: there were two gods, a good and an evil. Jesus was good but He was a good angel, the highest angel, not God and not man. These Albigensian heretics, who took their name from Albi in the south of France, one of their early strongholds, said that churches were evil and so were the sacraments, including marriage. Believers were assured of salvation by receiving a rite on their death-beds which included placing St John's Gospel on their heads. After that they received no food, starving to death or sometimes taking poison. Obviously the heresy was something which the Church just had to combat. Dominic did this by preaching. Unfortunately the Pope sought to put down the heresy by a crusade or holy war against the heretics, which began in 1209 and went on for twenty years, and in the course of which great atrocities were committed. St Dominic's was the better way. He gathered round him a band of men; there were sixteen of them in 1215, when he sought the sanction of the Pope, Innocent III, for his new order.

Innocent hesitated at first but afterwards yielded, and Honorius III, who succeeded him, gave them the title of Preaching Friars, *fratres praedicatores*. They were the Black Friars, so called from the black mantle which they wore over a white habit. As preachers whose special task was to convert heretics, the Dominicans were from the first a learned order, but like the Franciscans they begged their bread. Before St Dominic died at Bologna in 1221 the Dominicans were established in many parts of Europe, and by that same year they had landed in England.[1]

THE FRIARS IN ENGLAND

Both orders were in England before the deaths of their founders. Thirteen Dominicans, led by Gilbert de Fresnay, probably an Englishman, landed in 1221 and were welcomed by Peter des Roches, Bishop of Winchester, who took them to Canterbury. In twenty years they had established nineteen friaries, at such centres as York, Lincoln, Norwich, Bristol, Oxford, Cambridge, Northampton, and London. By 1300 the number had risen to fifty-one. By that date there were fifty-five Franciscan friaries, often in the same towns as the Dominican. The Franciscans had come in 1224, three of the nine friars who landed being of English birth, and five being laymen. St Francis himself was a layman. Throughout the thirteenth century the friars were the most vital spiritual force in this country, doing a great deal of good. Of the two great orders the Franciscans were always the more successful, partly because there was at the time no real heresy in England for the Dominicans to put down. Wiclif and the Lollards came a century later and by then the friars had fallen away. But there were always the ignorant to teach and the sick and dying to tend. Friars tended the lepers and in the frequent pestilences won great honour.

THE FRIARS AS MISSIONARIES

Here we reach their greatest glory; though this applies more particularly to the Franciscans, at least in the early days. St Francis himself visited the Holy Land and attempted to convert

[1] St Dominic has sometimes been called the first Inquisitor. But it seems that the Inquisition was not set up by him and was not active until ten years after his death. "We have no direct evidence that St Dominic ever condemned any single heretic; we know only that he received many back into the household of the Faith." See A. L. Maycock: *The Inquisition*, pp. 84, 85.

the Sultan of Egypt. This is how Miss Deanesly sums up their missionary labours. "The Franciscans worked from 1220 onwards in Morocco, Libya, Tunis and Algiers, many of them meeting death on their travels, and at the hands of the heathen. They preached, and founded convents and houses for pilgrims in the Holy Land and Egypt: in 1292 two Franciscans sailed round Africa with Genoese merchants, and in the fifteenth century they preached in Cape Verde, Guinea, and the Congo. They preached on the heathen borders of Europe, Lithuania, Poland and Prussia, and in the borderlands where the Greek church already struggled with the heathen or the Turk: Armenia, Bulgaria, and round the Black Sea and the Caspian. The work was not done without many martyrdoms. . . . They passed along merchant routes through Armenia and central Asia to Persia, India, Sumatra, Java, Borneo, Tibet and China."[1]

A young Franciscan from Italy, John of Monte Corvino, got to Peking. He had been on a mission to Persia when, on his return in 1289, the Pope sent him back to the East. From Persia he passed into India, where his companion, a Dominican, died. At length he reached China, where he found Nestorian Christians. (It is interesting in passing to note here that a Christian monk from Peking, visiting Europe, had already in 1287 had an audience with Edward I of England at Bordeaux. He had been entertained by the Pope, allowed to make his communion at the papal Mass and to celebrate his own. At Bordeaux Edward I was among his communicants. His name was Rabban Sauma, and although he was a Nestorian no one seems to have suspected his orthodoxy.) John considered the Nestorians imperfect Christians, and they strongly resented his coming. Perhaps that was natural. However, John laboured in Peking for forty years until his death; and for eleven years without a companion. Then Arnold of Cologne joined him. We know about him because in 1307 he got some Venetian merchants to carry a letter home. By that year he had a church which he had built six years previously; he had baptized some six thousand persons, bought one after another forty boys, sons of pagans, whom he had taught to sing the services, and had translated the New Testament, and the Psalter into the Tartar language. The Pope, when the letter was read to him, had seven Franciscans consecrated as bishops to join John, whom they were to consecrate as their archbishop. The mission continued until Christianity was put down in China by the

[1] M. Deanesly: *A History of the Medieval Church*, pp. 163, 164 (orig. ed.)

hostile Ming dynasty. All the Franciscan missionaries were martyred in 1362.

THE CRUSADES

We come now to a complete contrast. In the century preceding the founding of the friars the Crusades had brought Europe into closer touch with the East and given the peoples of the West a new and extended view of the world. They opened up the Mediterranean to trade and brought much wealth to Venice and other cities of the West. They did not bring Christianity to the East; their aim was never to convert the Moslems but to restore to Christianity the Holy Places.

The first four Crusades practically spanned the twelfth century; the following century is the great century of the friars. There was perhaps at the outset some excuse for taking up arms. The Arabs had been tolerant, and Byzantines and Arabs had found a way of living side by side. There was little religious strife and Christian pilgrims were welcomed in the Holy Land. But in 1055 the Seljuk Turks, who had crossed the Oxus a few years before, took Baghdad, and within twenty years had overrun Syria and Palestine. They had not long been Moslems. In 1071 the imperial army suffered the most decisive defeat in Byzantine history at Manzikert in Armenia at the hands of Alp Arslan, and the same year a Turkish adventurer Atsiz captured Jerusalem without a struggle and soon occupied nearly the whole of Palestine. The Fatimids of Egypt, who then ruled the Holy Land, recovered Jerusalem only to lose it again to Atsiz and suffer a massacre of the Moslem inhabitants. "Only the Christians, safe within their walled quarter, were spared." Atsiz was murdered and a Turkish prince, Tutush, ruled Palestine, showing "no special animosity . . . against the Christians"; nevertheless the two Orthodox Patriarchs of Antioch and Jerusalem seem to have preferred to spend their time in Constantinople. For a time the West stood in real danger and the Eastern Empire was nearly wrecked; and, if access to the East was not exactly forbidden to pilgrims, prevailing conditions made pilgrimage impossible. Then, in 1085, not only was the danger stayed by the defeat of the Turkish Sultan Suleiman ibn-Kutulmish by the Arabs of Aleppo, but new heart was put into the Christian West by successes against the Moslems in Spain. Toledo and northern Spain were won, and in 1091 the Normans completed their conquest of Sicily after a thirty years' struggle. The question was, could the Holy Land be recaptured?

We need not doubt the perfectly good motives behind the proclamation of the first Crusade by Pope Urban II in 1095, when "the whole world . . . desired to go to the tomb of our Lord in Jerusalem" and crowds flocked to take the Crusader's oath and to sew a cross of red material on the shoulder of their surcoat. But the Pope had "launched a movement greater than he knew. It might have been better if fewer great lords had answered his appeal. For, though with all of them except Bohemond [who secured possession of Antioch after its long siege by the Crusading army] genuine religious fervour was the strongest motive, soon their terrestrial schemes and rivalries would create troubles far beyond the papal legate's control. Still more uncontrollable was the response shown by humbler folk throughout France and Flanders and the Rhineland."[1]

Some were so eager that they started off on their own, to perish on the way. A People's Crusade, led by Peter the Hermit, met with disaster soon after entering Asia Minor, while Peter was in Constantinople, when thousands lost their lives. A German Crusade began by the massacre of Jews in Europe, a thousand being slaughtered at Mainz alone. It met a fate which many Christians thought that it deserved on the borders of Hungary, where the Hungarians, seriously alarmed, would not let the Crusaders pass. They were utterly routed and most of them slain. Up to this time the Jews had never been seriously persecuted in Europe, except long before in Visigothic Spain. Their position now worsened generally.

What of the main body of Crusaders, who at last, after incredible suffering and many set-backs, took Jerusalem in 1099 and next year set up a Latin kingdom there? No doubt to march an army from France overland through Asia Minor to Jerusalem, to defeat the Turks and their Egyptian allies and establish a chain of Christian states along the coast and inland as far as Edessa was an achievement of the first magnitude[2]; but the Crusaders had plundered, murdered and burned on the way, and how unlike was the taking of Jerusalem to that day in 638 when the Caliph Omar had entered the city. "The massacre at Jerusalem profoundly impressed all the world. No one can say how many victims it involved; but it emptied Jerusalem of its Moslem and Jewish inhabitants. Many even of the Christians

---

[1] S. Runciman: *A History of the Crusade*, vol. i, p. 113. Most of the quotations in this section are from this book.

[2] Cf. Christopher Dawson: *Religion and the Rise of Western Culture*, p. 178.

were horrified by what had been done. . . . It was this blood-thirsty proof of Christian fanaticism that recreated the fanaticism of Islam. When, later, wiser Latins in the East sought to find some basis on which Christian and Moslem could work together, the memory of the massacre stood always in the way." [1] Those who stood to lose most were the native, non-Latin Christians of the East.

The second Crusade came half a century later and was occasioned by the danger in which the Latin kingdoms stood from the Moslems of Mosul. There had been trouble between the western Crusaders and their Greek allies on the first Crusade; now relations between them were as bad as they could be. The Crusade collapsed, the western leaders abandoning those whom they had led and sailing home from Attalia.

In 1187 Saladin took Jerusalem. The third Crusade was an unsuccessful attempt to retake it. It was on this Crusade that Richard Cœur-de-Lion went. Richard refortified Acre (which remained the Crusaders' last stronghold in Syria till it fell to the Turks in 1291), and made a truce with Saladin. In 1191 he took the Greek island of Cyprus, where a revolution was in progress, and sold it to Guy de Lusignan, the ex-king of Jerusalem, who established a dynasty there. The island became the base of the military orders of the Knights of St John of Jerusalem and the Templars, and a centre from which to continue the struggle against the Moslems.

But the fourth Crusade (1202–4) was the most disgraceful of all. Pope Innocent III had intended it to attack Egypt. The Venetians, to whom the transport of Crusaders had proved very profitable, secured that instead it should attack Constantinople, which was fabulous for its treasures. A dynastic quarrel afforded an excuse to intervene, and a massacre of Latins in Constantinople twenty years before (1182) invited reprisals. By an arrangement the French and the Venetians were to share equally in the booty, and on April 13th, 1204, the city was taken and for three days was given over to pillage. Scenes of almost incredible brutality and sacrilege followed. St Sophia saw the destruction of sacred books and treasures by the drunken soldiery who tore the jewels from the altars: murder, robbery and rape were rife. Even the Saracens, the Greek historian Nicetas said, would have been more merciful. A Latin emperor, Baldwin, Count of Flanders, was crowned in St Sophia and a Venetian made Patriarch of Constantinople. It goes

[1] Runciman, *op. cit.*, p. 287.

without saying that when the Greeks re-entered the city in 1261 (for the Latin Empire collapsed after half a century) the two Churches were farther apart than ever before. The memory of 1204 "burnt deep into the Eastern mind and it was the behaviour of the Crusaders more than any other single circumstance which made the breach between East and West permanent." [1]

[1] R. M. French: *The Eastern Orthodox Church*, pp. 77, 78.

Learning and Devotion: Schoolmen and Poets

One who disapproved of the Crusades as a wicked and useless waste of time was the English Franciscan friar, Roger Bacon (*c.* 1214–*c.* 1292). An Elizabethan playwright, Robert Greene, was destined one day to write *The Honourable History of Friar Bacon and Friar Bungay*, in which he would weave together a number of different worlds in much the same way that Shakespeare was to do in *A Midsummer Night's Dream*. One was the world of magic. The play is not exactly history, nor is it much about Friar Bungay, but Friar Bacon is the Roger Bacon who deplored the Crusades, who studied at Oxford, though not at Brasenose College, which did not then exist, and whose fame as a magician had become legendary. There are scenes of magic laid in Bacon's rooms in "Brazen-nose". But we are introduced as well to the world of the court and to the Suffolk countryside and Margaret, the game-keeper's daughter. There is a charming love story of Margaret and Lacy, Earl of Lincoln, who, sent to woo her on behalf of the Prince of Wales, woos and wins her for himself. And in Oxford the Prince sees through a marvellous "glass prospective"

what's done in merry Fressingfield
'Twixt lovely Peggy and the Lincoln Earl.

(Presumably the Suffolk scene would be acted on the inner stage.) However, the Prince is magnanimous enough to give up Margaret to Lacy. Near the end of the play a brazen head is shown, on which Bacon has laboured for seven years. It speaks three times—"Time is", "Time was", "Time is past"—before there is a flash of lightning and a hand appears and breaks it in pieces with a hammer.

BACON AND EXPERIMENTAL SCIENCE

Here is something which was written a long way from Oxford, where Bacon had studied under one of the greatest of medieval churchmen, Robert Grosseteste, afterwards Bishop of Lincoln, and from Paris, where Bacon joined the Franciscan order, for he was not a friar while at Oxford. It was written at Zara in Dalmatia, in 1385, by a certain Paul of Trau:

"Friar Roger, called Bacon, an Englishman, intent rather on practical philosophy than on writing it, performed wonderful experiments . . . By natural condensation (of the air) he made a bridge thirty miles long over the sea from the Continent to England, and, after passing over it safely with all his retinue destroyed it by rarefying the air by natural means."

Bacon is not credited by Paul, however absurd the latter's views, with making the bridge by magic. He makes and destroys it by natural, i.e. scientific, means. Another extract from the same writer brings us back to Greene's play:

"He (Bacon) was so complete a master of optics that from love of experiment he neglected teaching and writing, and made two mirrors in the University of Oxford: by one of them you could light a candle at any hour, day or night; in the other you could see what people were doing in any part of the world. By experimenting with the first, students spent more time in lighting candles than studying books; and seeing, in the second, their relations dying or ill or otherwise in trouble, they got into the habit of going down, to the ruin of the University; so by common council of the University both mirrors were broken." [1]

Bacon wrote more than these extracts would suggest, although not (so far as we know) in his Oxford days; and one thing which he laments is the very little attention being given to the study of optics. In his *Opus Majus*, written at the command of his friend Pope Clement IV, who overrode the prohibition of his Franciscan superior, who sought to muzzle him, Bacon gives a long description of the structure of the human eye; and there he repeats the opinion that Julius Caesar used something like a telescope to see Britain from the coast of Gaul. It is possible that he did himself invent a telescope; he certainly knew that lenses might be used as aids to vision.

He was always pleading for "more and better scientific

[1] Both extracts are quoted from A. G. Little's British Academy Lecture on *Roger Bacon*, 1928, by F. Winthrop Woodruff in his popular biography, *Roger Bacon* (p. 14.)

investigation" (to quote a modern writer), and that in all sorts of fields. For example, he believed that the world was round; and his knowledge of astronomy told him that the Julian calendar then in use was inaccurate. He says that "Julius did not arrive at the true length of the year"; he was out by one day in about a hundred and thirty years. And over the course of time that mounted up. He says that "the corruption of the calendar . . . is intolerable to all wisdom, the horror of all astronomy"; surely "none perceiving such an abomination could allow it to go on." But it went on, for another three hundred years, and in England the reformed Gregorian calendar was not officially adopted till 1752. This, however, shows the kind of man the real Bacon was. If like most men of his day he believed in the influence of the stars, for him astrology was a branch of astronomy and here as elsewhere experiment was the ultimate test.

We need not be surprised that some things which he accepted on hearsay evidence seem to us childish; he belonged to his own age though in many ways he was centuries in advance of it. But in one respect he has a lesson for us. While he believed in experimental science he never thought that it could take the place of true religion. And to religion he brought the same qualities that he showed as a scientist. He was a good Biblical scholar and knew Hebrew and Greek as well as Latin. Observation told him that the Latin Bible then in use was inaccurate in places, due to copyists' mistakes. So we find him pleading for a revised and more accurate text. It was, again, some three hundred years before a revised, authoritative, text was published.

We can see how the Bacon legend grew up. But we do not know how the brazen head came to be attributed to him: nothing in his writings suggests it. Bacon in fact believed that sorcery was either fraudulent or a delusion. In this, too, he was much in advance of his age. That he was put in prison for fourteen years *propter novitates*, "on account of novelties", will not surprise us.

THE SCHOOLMEN

Bacon's life spans most of the thirteenth century (*c.* 1214– *c.* 1292). This was the age when the universities were developing: they had begun in the previous century. In Italy Bologna was already famous as a law school; and Paris had developed the study of theology. Oxford went back to the time of Henry II, Cambridge to soon after the turn of the century. A famous teacher in Paris in the first days of the university was Peter Abelard (1079–1142), a native of Brittany. He is one of the early Schoolmen, men whose aim was to reconcile faith and reason. St Anselm, who lived before the days of universities, is often regarded as the first Schoolman. Anselm said: *Credo ut intelligam*, I believe in order that I may understand. That is to say, for him Christian belief lit up everything else. Abelard allowed the pre-eminence of faith, but held that knowledge comes first, since men believe from conviction. He would have said: I understand in order that I may believe.

St Anselm called his principal work *Cur Deus Homo?* "Why did God become Man?" The Nicene Creed puts the reason in two little words: "who *for us* men, and for our salvation came down from heaven. . . . And was made man. And was crucified also *for us*." Writers and teachers have constantly sought to draw out what those two little words imply. St Anselm found the answer in the satisfaction which God required on account of man's sin. Only a sinless life, a life of perfect obedience, could outweigh the dishonour done to God by sin, so Christ came to do *for us* what we could not do for ourselves. Abelard said that Christ came to show the love of God and so win man's response, to kindle an answering love. That is certainly one reason but the "for us" of the Creed can hardly mean no more than that.

This is not the place to discuss the Atonement, but what we want to be quite clear about is that the subjects which occupied the early Schoolmen were not things which do not matter.

Peter Lombard (1100–1164) was another Schoolman. He wrote a kind of summary of Theology, a book called the *Sentences*, which set out the doctrines of the Church methodically and was used as a text-book by students right up to the Reformation. Luther lectured on it and always retained a respect for it. But greater than Peter Lombard was St Thomas Aquinas (1227–1274), whose greatest work—of which the modern printed editions go into many volumes—is simply called *The Sum of Theology* (*Summa Theologiae*). From the age of five he was brought up at the monastery of Monte Cassino, where he kept asking the question "What is God?" In his sixteenth year he entered the Dominican order and soon became the pupil of a famous German Schoolman, also a Dominican, Albert the Great, at Cologne, and then at Paris. When St Thomas died, in his forty-eighth year, the *Summa Theologica* was still unfinished. It is in three parts—the first treating of God, the second of man, and the third (unfinished) part of our

Lord and the Sacraments. What is remarkable is the clear and systematic way in which St Thomas divides up his subject and each question he deals with. He states objections always fairly and meets them. He quotes authorities—the Scriptures, the Fathers, or it may be Aristotle, whose philosophy was only then being accepted in the Christian schools; but he always also reasons things out himself. St Thomas Aquinas is looked upon as *the* philosopher to this day by the Roman Catholic Church.

HYMNS OF DEVOTION

We all have a means of getting to know quite a lot about St Thomas Aquinas, and this not by studying his philosophy, but from his hymns. He was not only a Schoolman but a mystic and a poet. His devotion to our Lord, especially to our Lord in the Blessed Sacrament of the altar, comes out clearly in his hymns,

Now, my tongue the mystery telling. . . .

The Heavenly Word proceeding forth. . . .

Thee we adore, O hidden Saviour, Thee. . . .

Anyone who attends a sung Eucharist will certainly know the second part of the first two hymns: "Therefore we, before Him bending", and "O Saving Victim, opening wide." The originals are in rhymed Latin but they have been translated into the same rhythms in English so that we can still sing them to the same plainsong melodies. The same is true of Abelard's glorious *O quanta, qualia sunt illa sabbata,* "Oh, what the joy and the glory must be"—originally written to be sung on Saturday evening.

THE VISION OF PIERS THE PLOWMAN

We have no one in England to match Dante, who was far and away the greatest poet of the Middle Ages. "The nearest approach to Dante in our poetry," says Dr B. Ifor Evans in the Pelican *Short History of English Literature,* is William Langland, who "despite his roughness . . . has written the greatest poem in English devoted to the Christian way of life." [1] The meaning of *Piers Plowman* is the quest for God, a quest in three stages, which the poet calls *Do-Well, Do-Better* and *Do-Best.* The first is the active life of honest labour (with the fear of God in one's heart and a love of one's neighbour). This we can all understand and most people never get beyond this. But Langland did not believe there was nothing higher than this. *Do-Better* is the life of contemplative love, of prayer and renunciation; in a

[1] *Op. cit.* p. 20.

word, the monastic life. Langland has scathing things to say
about monks but never about the monastic ideal. Yet, as Professor R. W. Chambers says, "there is a still higher ideal. The
man who has renounced all may be called back into active life,
to rule and direct others. The episcopal ideal is higher than the
monastic or clerkly ideal: it is *Do-Best.*"[1]

MYSTERY AND MIRACLE PLAYS, MORALITIES AND CAROLS

A line or two of *Piers Plowman* will appear in the next chapter,
but to do justice to a poem on the Christian way of life it
should be quoted at length and that is impossible. Nor can we
quote from the mystery and miracle plays which began our
native drama and belong in the main to the fourteenth century,
though they were still being acted well in the reign of Elizabeth
I.[2] They "gave to the people of England a taste for theatrical
shows; they prepared the ground for the Elizabethan drama"—
but they grew out of the Church's liturgical worship, particularly that at the Easter season, when as far back as Saxon times
there was a simple dramatization in church of the scene at the
Empty Tomb, the coming of the women and the message of the
angel, *Non est hic, surrexit sicut praedixerat,* "He is not here,
He has risen even as He said before." The mystery and miracle
plays, in which devotion and comedy, high seriousness, satire
and sometimes coarseness, were all mixed up together, are in this
completely typical of the Middle Ages as they are in their
anachronisms and their anonymity. The York cycle is the most
complete, with forty-eight plays and a fragment, each allocated
to a trade gild, the whole running through the story of man's
redemption from the Creation to the Judgement Day; but in
the thirteenth, fourteenth and fifteenth centuries these plays
are known to have been acted in over one hundred and twenty-
five towns and villages in England, Wales and Scotland, and at

[1] *Man's Unconquerable Mind*, p. 103. See chs. 4 and 5 for an illuminating
discussion of the poem.
[2] "At Coventry in 1573 a certain Fawson received from one of the
companies fourpence 'for hangying Judas' and fourpence 'for Coc
croyng'" (Allardyce Nicoll: *British Drama*, p. 27). This was only some
fifteen or sixteen years before Greene wrote his *Honourable History of
Friar Bacon and Friar Bungay*. There was a technical distinction between
mysteries and miracle plays; mysteries dealt with themes from the Bible
and miracle plays with the lives of saints; but the terms have now become
practically synonymous.

Dublin and Kilkenny as well.[1] They were acted out of doors, usually on movable stages, called "pageants", and it is quite clear that the Church authorities viewed them with some misgiving, even though they were part of the Corpus Christi celebrations. The morality plays, such as *Everyman*, were more professional; these were not, like the mysteries, the entertainment of the masses but plays written to be performed indoors, in the halls of the gentry. They have as the *dramatis personae* allegorial characters, and belong to the fifteenth and sixteenth centuries.

Then, too, so much of the lyric verse of the Middle Ages was religious. The fifteenth century was the great century for carols. And what lovely carols many of them are! Most exquisite of all, surely, is this carol from the anonymous Sloane MS. 2593 in the British Museum:[2]

> I sing of a maiden
>> That is makëles (matchless),
> King of all Kinges
>> To her sone sche ches (chose).
> He cam also (all so) stille
>> There his moder was,
> As dew in Aprille
>> That falleth on the grass.
> He cam also stille
>> To his moderës bour,
> As dew in Aprille
>> That falleth on the flour.
> He cam also stille
>> There his moder lay,
> As dew in Aprille
>> That falleth on the spray.
> Moder and maiden
>> Was never non but sche;
> Well may swich a lady
>> Godës moder be.

[1] *British Drama*, p. 29.

[2] A very slightly modernized version appears in the *Oxford Book of Carols*, No. 183. The original form, as above, is given in *Early English Lyrics*, ed. Chambers and Sidgwick.

19

Why a Reformation?

THE FOURTEENTH AND FIFTEENTH CENTURIES

The two centuries which preceded the Reformation were a time of a general lowering of moral standards.

> The greater part of this people that pass their way on earth
> Have their honour in this world and wish for nothing better,
> Of other heaven than here holding no opinion.

So says William Langland.[1] But we should make a mistake if we imagined that religious observance was neglected. Not everyone went to church though most people did, especially in the towns. You would have found the ordinary citizen in his parish church not only on Sundays and at service-time but at other times for his private prayers. The daily prayers which we say at home, he would have said in church. Books would not have been provided, but those who could provided themselves with them. They were certainly used. Printing was invented about half-way through the fifteenth century and Caxton set up the first printing-press in England in 1476. Before the introduction of printing, when all books had to be copied by hand, they were naturally more difficult to come by, and also more expensive. Rather more than half the population, at least in the towns, could read. The fifteenth century did quite a lot for education: there were chantry and gild schools, in the towns of course. We can be sure that copies of the *Lay Folks' Mass Book* and the *Prymer* were taken into the churches. The *Prymer* contained a variety of devotions and you could get a copy in English, or one with English and Latin on opposite pages. Devotion to the Blessed Virgin was very common and you would find such devotions as the Hours of our Lady; but you would also find, e.g. the penitential psalms. (These are Nos. 6 (against anger), 32 (pride), 38 (gluttony), 51 (lust), 102 (avarice), 130 (envy), 143 (sloth).) On Sundays and other days when you heard Mass you would take with you the *Lay Folks' Mass Book* with its

[1] *Visions from Piers Plowman*, tr. by N. Coghill, p. 21. Perhaps it is always so.

paraphrases in English and in verse of parts of the service. Conduct might lag behind devotion, but people were devout. They accepted the Faith with very little questioning, and with it also a good deal of superstition.

There is no evidence that people were falling away from religious practice because of the abuses that had grown up, or that they wanted a drastic revision of the services. Most of them wanted the services left as they were. The Reformation did not come about because the laity were smouldering with discontent which suddenly flared up and demanded reform. When it came in the sixteenth century its earliest leaders were monks and clergymen. Those two earlier heralds of reform, John Wiclif and John Huss, were both of them clergymen. Wiclif, who spent most of his life as a teacher at Oxford, when he died in 1384 was still Rector of Lutterworth in Leicestershire (where the chasuble he wore is still shown). John Huss of Prague, through whom the teachings of Wiclif took firmer hold in Bohemia than in England in spite of the Lollards, was also both a priest and a university teacher. The Council of Constance burnt Huss as a heretic in 1415 and condemned Wiclif, whose body was disinterred, burnt and thrown in the river. Langland, who was a contemporary of Wiclif and Chaucer, was in minor orders, and it is quite clear from their poetry that Langland was much more concerned about the abuses which were rife in the Church than was the layman Chaucer. Chaucer could laugh at the monk who was everything a monk ought not to be; who didn't stay in his cloister, didn't work with his hands, or study, but who kept hounds and loved hunting and "a fat swan . . . best of any roast"; he could even agree with him, speaking perhaps with his tongue in his cheek: "And I said his opinion was good." What would Langland, long Will, have said? He might have found here the kind of monk who was laying up in store the retribution which, he said, would one day come through an English king, who would punish the religious orders for breaking the rule of poverty and asceticism and would give the Abbot of Abingdon a fatal knock on the crown. It reads like a prophecy, except that the aim of the king was to lead the monks back to old and better ways. We must not think of Langland as a Protestant before his time; but he was acutely aware of the desperate need of reform and renewal in the Church of his day. Most of the medieval abuses could have been rectified and western Christendom could still have remained a unity, had not the papacy itself been the real stumbling-block.

ABUSES

What were the abuses that needed rectifying? Here are some of the more obvious ones.

1. The laziness and immoral lives of *some* of the clergy. Langland speaks of Parson Sloth, of the unprofitable lives of many of the friars, of the "hermits a heap" who went to Walsingham, "and their wenches after (them)"; but he also says that *many* chaplains were chaste, *many* parish priests kept themselves pure in body, and he would not have said so if it had not been true.

2. Avariciousness. The impression one gets is that the Church *as a whole* cared far too much for money. The legal officers necessitated by the church courts were grasping and venal. Among Chaucer's pilgrims the most unattractive character of all is the Summoner, whom the poet describes without a touch of sympathy. But avarice had attacked the clergy too. Chaucer's Friar who gave an easy penance and taught that

> instead of weeping and prayers
> Men must give silver to the poor friars,

and Langland's "parsons and parish priests" who left their livings to sing as chantry priests in London, did what they did "for (because) silver is sweet". Yet there is the other side. Livings were often miserably poor and the average vicar's pay, about £4 a year, was rather less than the average artisan's, not withstanding that out of it he must pay a curate and the parish clerk, pay for repairs and renewals in the church, and meet the calls of hospitality. About half the livings had become vicarages by the end of the thirteenth century, through the appropriation of so many of them to the monasteries. The monasteries then became the rectors and took the big tithe. There was the even worse scandal of appointing the sons of noble houses, or of large land-owners, to livings, often to many livings held in plurality, the duties of which they never intended to perform. But as rectors they drew the emoluments, employing a cheap deputy to perform the ministrations; while they themselves might be in no more than minor orders, though they were supposed to be at least deacons.

3. The luxury and display of the monks and the higher clergy. We have seen that most monasteries employed a whole army of servants. Dr Owst tells this story. A great theologian preached one Palm Sunday about our Lord's humility and the ass. Afterwards, when he mounted his richly caparisoned palfrey, an old

hag hung on the bridle, saying, "Master, was our Lord's ass like that?"[1] There is no doubt that the Church was too wealthy and that bishops were often worldly.

4. Superstitious practices. One was the veneration of relics. As we saw in an earlier chapter this cult came in from the East at a comparatively early date. Constantinople was the great home of relics. But they were common throughout Christendom. Frederick the Wise, Elector of Saxony, the protector of Luther, had got together a vast collection of seventeen thousand four hundred and forty-three relics in the Castle Church at Wittenberg by the year following the nailing of his ninety-five theses by Luther on the church door. They included two hundred and four portions and one complete corpse of the Holy Innocents![2] The fashion of going on pilgrimages gave occasion for abuses of various kinds, as well as for fraud. Erasmus, who visited Walsingham—a house of Augustinian canons and the most famous shrine of our Lady in England—in 1513 (the same year as Henry VIII's queen, Catherine of Aragon, who paid her visit in thanksgiving for the victory of Flodden), was bold enough to ask what was the evidence that the concreted milk of the Holy Virgin was really her milk, and had further doubts about other things as well. Walsingham was the most disorderly house in England. The invocation of saints was carried to extreme lengths, especially devotion to the Blessed Virgin. Men approached her in preference to her Son: she was the more certain to show pity, and could she not still command Christ as His mother? The story of the vision of two ladders was told. "They stretched to heaven. Our Lord leant over the top of one, His mother over the other. Those who tried to ascend by the red one to our Lord often fell off into hell. All those who ascended by the white one were received into heaven by our Lady."[3]

5. The Inquisition. This was first set up in the middle of the thirteenth century *after* the Emperor Frederick Barbarossa had enacted a law decreeing burning or the cutting out of the tongue as the penalty for heresy. We should notice here that burnings belong to the *later* Middle Ages. The first burning of heretics was at Orleans in 1022, as a result of a "sort of extraordinary general meeting" summoned by King Robert the Pious. Before the eleventh century the death penalty had only once been

[1] G. R. Owst: *Preaching in Medieval England*, p. 210.
[2] G. Rupp: *Luther's Progress to the Diet of Worms*, 1521, p. 52.
[3] H. Maynard Smith: *Pre-Reformation England*, p. 160.

applied in the West to heretics—by the Emperor Maximus in 385, when the Spaniard Priscillian and six companions, one a woman, were put to death on a charge of magic. There was a storm of protest, in which St Ambrose at Milan, St Martin of Tours and Pope Siricius joined. St Augustine of Hippo, though prepared to allow a "temperate severity" in dealing with obstinate heretics, did not allow the death penalty. The worst horrors of the Inquisition arrived very late on the pre-Reformation scene. The Inquisition never gained a footing in England, the Scandinavian countries or Portugal; and not in Spain until Ferdinand and Isabella established the Spanish Inquisition in 1480. Here it was seen at its very worst. It is horrible to think that the Church should have used torture, yet the civil law including that of England sanctioned it, and the reformers themselves put to death those whose opinions were held to be subversive of the true faith. This was done with a will in Calvinist Geneva. Cruelty was a blot on the Middle Ages and it did not cease when they came to an end. But the damage done by the Inquisition lay not only in the cruelty practised but in the attempt to stifle inquiry and the search for truth.

6. Indulgences: the Pardoners. The Church taught that while absolution forgave sins the punishment which they entailed had to be paid either by doing penance in this world or by suffering in Purgatory. But a practice arose by which you could be let off some of the penance (e.g. so many days on bread and water), or in certain circumstances the whole of it, if you gave alms. Only the Pope could grant a plenary or full indulgence. This was first granted in connexion with the first Crusade. Popes found in the sale of indulgences a useful means of raising money and the whole practice became a dreadful scandal. Indulgences were hawked round by pardoners, who were usually attached to some hospital (which would be a home of relics), and though many of them were laymen they had permission to preach at Mass. Usually indulgences cost fourpence, sometimes only a penny. Fraud was common. None of their contemporaries have a good word to say for the pardoners and in the end they were suppressed. With their wallets "Bret-ful (brim-full) of pardon come from Rome all hot", they take us straight to the greatest scandal of all, the Papacy itself.

7. The Papacy. The decline began half-way through the thirteenth century, not long after the great days of Innocent III. "The papacy . . . ceased to be religious." A papal secretary wrote of the papal court: "they talk every day of castles, lands,

cities, of all kinds of war weapons, of money," but not of religion; it was "worldly, devilish, despotic", worse than any secular court.[1] Some of the popes were not only worldly but wicked; and even a good pope wanted money. It was the papal demands for money that aroused the first anti-papal feeling in this country in the reign of Henry III. That the clergy found most of it did not mean that the laity did not bitterly resent the demands. (Of the papal taxes only Peter's Pence, a very small tax, was paid by the laity.)

THE "BABYLONISH CAPTIVITY" AND THE GREAT SCHISM

In 1305 the French king, Philip the Fair, secured the election of a French pope, Clement V. Clement transferred the papacy to France, first to Lyons, then in 1309 to Avignon where it remained up to 1377. This was the time of the Hundred Years' War with France. Money collected for the papacy was bound to benefit England's enemy. So anti-papal feeling became mixed up with anti-French feeling.

John Wiclif (*c.* 1320–84) was strongly nationalist. But he desired reform for religious reasons. He was not opposed to the idea of a papacy, nor did he think that its centre need be Rome, but he held that the Pope should resemble Christ and that deadly sin had lost to the papacy any right to levy tribute under the promise made by King John. It is interesting to notice that he himself was not appointed to a canonry at Lichfield, which he was promised in 1373, because he refused to pay the first year's income to the Pope. A foreigner was appointed in his place. Here we have an example of two of the principal ways by which the papal revenues were kept going. One was the system of annates, by which the Popes claimed the right to take the "first year's fruit" or revenue from certain benefices, which by 1400 had become the vast majority. The same applied to bishoprics. The other was the claim to "provide" to benefices, overriding local patrons. By this means foreign ecclesiastics were put into livings, of which they drew the incomes but which they never visited. It was a way of paying the papal staff! Both these abuses increased during the seventy years' sojourn at Avignon, when the Popes needed money more than ever—partly because they kept up a more luxurious state. This, the "Babylonish Captivity", as the Italian Petrarch called it, did harm to the papacy, and the Great Schism which followed it did more harm still.

---

[1] Quoted by G. J. Jordan: *The Inner History of the Great Schism*, p. 27.

Why a Reformation?

In 1377 Gregory XI left Avignon for Rome, to the dismay of his cardinals who much preferred Avignon. But Gregory died the next year and the new Pope was elected with the populace shouting "We want a Roman or at least an Italian." The cardinals elected a Neapolitan who became Urban VI. But very soon they complained of the heat and got permission to reside at Anagni. Then they declared the election null and void on the ground that they had been intimidated. They elected another Pope, Clement VII. But two days before the election Urban had created twenty-six new cardinals to take their places, and he promptly excommunicated the rival Pope. Clement however set sail with his cardinals for Marseilles and re-established the papacy at Avignon. From now on for some forty years there were two Popes and two colleges of cardinals; some parts of Europe acknowledged one and some the other, England following the Urbanist line, Scotland and France the Clementine. There was complete bewilderment when Urbanists and Clementines were found side by side; at Bruges the Urbanist population refused to hear Mass said by Clementine priests and went to Ghent to make their Easter communion.

THE CONCILIAR MOVEMENT

How could this state of affairs be ended? One suggestion was that one or both Popes should abdicate, but neither would. Then the way of a General Council was popularized; only hitherto in the West, General Councils had always been called by the Pope. It was claimed that necessity overrode this, and the peace of the Church and the good of Christendom demanded that some way out be found. In the end both sets of cardinals deserted their Popes, fled to Pisa and summoned a Council largely of prelates which met there in 1409. This council failed because neither the Roman Pope nor the Avignon Pope who were deposed, would acknowledge their deposition and all the council did was to elect yet another Pope: so now there were three. Nevertheless it paved the way for the solution. The successor to the third Pope was prevailed upon by the Emperor, Sigismund, to call together another assembly, this time one of princes equally with ecclesiastics. This was the Council of Constance, which met from 1414 to 1418, and over which Sigismund presided. In November 1417 it elected Oddo Colonna as Pope Martin V, and restored unity to Western Christendom.

Unfortunately, however, the Renaissance Popes dragged the papacy down to its lowest depth of infamy. Their aim was not

149

religious, it was to build up the papal states into a strong principality; and their court became a byword for vice of every sort. Is it surprising that the one thing about which there was almost complete popular agreement at the Reformation was the repudiation of the Pope?

20

The Reformation Abroad : Luther

A NEW AGE

When the sixteenth century dawned new life was stirring in Europe. It was the age of the New Learning, which was really a return to the ideals of the classical past, the age of humanism. The centre was shifting from eternity to the present, from God to man. No earthly experience or enterprise or attainment seemed out of man's reach. The Italian Renaissance had begun before the fall of Constantinople to the Turks in 1453, but its capture, by hastening the flight of Greek scholars with their precious manuscripts across the Adriatic into Italy, gave impetus to the movement, and the invention of printing helped enormously. The rediscovery of Greek civilization provided a new and often pagan delight in life and the senses; it also gave a new feeling for form, which was to bear fruit in the revival of literature and a belief in the unfettered use of the human reason. The new age was one of scientific experiment and of philosophical inquiry. The geographical horizon was expanding also. The 1490s in particular—when Columbus discovered America, Cabot sighted Nova Scotia and Vasco da Gama rounded the Cape of Good Hope—were a decade of maritime exploration and the discovery of new lands. The Church could not but be affected.

MOVEMENTS OF REFORM—ERASMUS, XIMENES

Christianity was regarded with much more critical eyes than hitherto, but that does not mean that it was necessarily rejected. Erasmus of Rotterdam (1466–1536), probably the greatest of all the humanists, strove to make the New Learning serve the cause of religion. In a Latin work, the *Praise of Folly*, he laughed at follies of all kinds, and made Folly observe that there were no "enemies of the Church more pernicious than impious popes". He believed that Luther had done much good and was no heretic, but he could not countenance Luther's break with

151

Rome. Erasmus foresaw only too clearly—as few others did—
the consequences which must inevitably follow. The rising tide
of nationalism held dangers enough. To divide Christendom,
so far from serving as a check upon it, must carry an increased
danger of war. It was because the Pope valued his efforts for
peace as well as his scholarship, that he offered him, the year
before he died, a cardinal's hat, which Erasmus declined on the
score of age. His aim was reform within the Catholic Church.
It was because he believed that ignorance stood in the way of
reform that he brought out at Basle, in 1516, the first printed
Greek Testament.

From *The Church of our Fathers*

ERASMUS OF ROTTERDAM
(1466–1536)

In Spain there had been a movement of partial reform,
beginning before the turn of the century and carried through
largely by Cardinal Ximenes, Archbishop of Toledo. First, the
morals of the clergy were reformed. They needed reform though
they had not sunk to the level common in Italy. Then Ximenes
accomplished a revival of scholarship. His own monument to
fame is the *Complutensian Polyglot*, an edition of the Bible in
parallel columns, giving the Hebrew, Greek and Latin texts,
besides such "helps" as a Hebrew grammar and dictionary.
It was planned in 1502 but the six volumes did not appear till
1522. Unfortunately the Spanish Reformation was gravely
marred by the Inquisition.

MARTIN LUTHER (1483–1546)

When the break with Rome came it was Luther who played the decisive part. Yet he was no "modern", nor even a humanist like Erasmus. In many ways he was medieval and not least because for him God always stood at the centre, the One Being who had to be reckoned with. The Reformation affected politics and contributed in the economic sphere to the development of capitalistic speculation already well under way, but this was not by Luther's intention. No one cared less for the "spoils". There he was as unlike the German peasantry of the Peasants' War, "interested mainly in pillaging castles and cloisters", as he was unlike Henry VIII of England. The Church of the early Middle Ages "had bestowed the highest esteem on agriculture, next on handicraft, and last of all on commerce. This too was Luther's scale of values." [1]

Luther came of peasant stock. He was born in 1483 at Eisleben in Saxony, but his father removed to Mansfeld to work in the copper mines and eventually to become a town councillor. At seventeen Martin entered the university of Erfurt. After taking his master's degree at twenty-two, he began to study law. Then suddenly, the same year (1505), he entered the cloister, becoming an Austin Friar. The Augustinians had a house of seventy members at Erfurt. Luther believed he had received a call from heaven. Overtaken by a thunderstorm near Erfurt, a flash of lightning struck him to earth. He cried out in terror, "Help, St Anne, and I'll become a monk," (St Anne was the patron saint of miners.) He took a fortnight to put his affairs in order, then sought admission to the cloister. Next year he was professed as a friar and in 1507 ordained priest.

We must think of Luther as a good friar. He said years afterwards: "if the monastic life could get a man to heaven, I should have entered: all my companions who knew me will bear witness to that". "I vexed myself with fastings and prayers beyond what was common". [2] But if he had joined the Augustinians to find inner peace he did not find it. He felt he had failed dismally. He believed he had come under the wrath of God, who must be reconciled with good works.

It was Johann Staupitz, Vicar General of the order, who helped him most: partly by giving him sensible advice, still more in 1511, after Luther's return from his one visit to Rome

---

[1] Bainton: *Here I Stand*, p. 236.
[2] Quoted by G. Rupp: *Luther's Progress to the Diet of Worms*, pp. 26, 27.

where he was sent on a mission with another brother, by getting him transferred to Wittenberg to take his doctor's degree and to succeed Staupitz himself as professor of Biblical theology. This Luther did the next year, at the age of twenty-eight. For the rest of his life Wittenberg was his home. It was a very small town, and its university, the pride of the Elector Frederick the Wise, very new, unlike Erfurt; but Luther made Wittenberg a household word.[1] His duties lay not only in the classroom; he had also to preach, at first only in the monastery, but from 1514 in the town church, which became his special charge. His first course of lectures was on the Psalms. These of course he knew well, but up to that time he had made no systematic study of the Bible as a whole. He now did so until, as Mr Gordon Rupp observes, "his mind was drenched through and through with the Biblical material". His next course was on St Paul's Epistle to the Romans. But if he lectured mostly on the Epistles he preached mostly on the Gospels; and in helping others he helped himself, as Staupitz had evidently thought he would. He did this in the main by learning two things:

(1) that the righteous God is also merciful; he came to love the suffering Redeemer;
(2) that, on man's side, the one requisite is faith.

The last came to him in the tower of the monastery as he meditated on Romans 1. 16, 17. His fears were gone; he felt as though he had "gone through open doors to paradise". The doctrine of Justification by Faith, which means that our salvation comes from our faith in God who saves us, and is not something which has to be won by good works, was not really new but it came as something new to Luther.[2] What was new was to add the word *alone*, as Luther did when translating the New Testament into German; he said it required the addition to bring out the sense. This however makes "works" of no account; and yet Luther looked for good works on the part of the faithful.

THE QUESTION OF INDULGENCES

Luther's conflict with Rome did not come to a head very quickly, but it was obvious that one holding his view of faith

[1] Shakespeare makes Wittenberg Hamlet's university (*Hamlet*, Act I, scene 2).

[2] In theology "to be justified" is to be regarded in the eyes of God as "just" or "righteous".

as the one thing necessary would have no use for such things as indulgences or the superstitious veneration of relics. Frederick the Wise, as we have seen, had assembled a wonderful collection of relics of the saints at Wittenberg. They were displayed every year on All Saints' Day and in connexion with them the Pope had granted to the Castle Church the privilege of dispensing indulgences. They included the rare privilege of an indulgence granting full remission of all sins. Luther, who was in charge of the town parish, believed that the sale of indulgences imperilled his flock. So in 1516 on three occasions, when preaching in the Castle Church (the church for the university), he spoke critically of them. His case was that only true contrition can win the remission of sins; if you were truly contrite you did not need an indulgence, if you were not, to buy one only produced a false sense of security. He did not believe that Popes had the power to release souls from purgatory, as they had claimed to have since 1476 in the time of Sixtus IV. There were others who thought as Luther did; Erasmus was one.

In 1517 a particularly flagrant form of indulgence was issued, and though Frederick would not permit it to be offered in Electoral Saxony, it was sold across the border not far from Wittenberg and any Wittenberger who chose could buy one. John Tetzel, a Dominican, was the official vendor and in his sermons he made play with the jingle:

> As soon as the coin in the coffer rings,
> The soul from purgatory springs.

You could release a soul from purgatory without being yourself penitent, he said. The proceeds were supposed to go to the rebuilding of St Peter's Rome; actually the Pope had arranged for half to go to the young Archbishop of Mainz, Prince Albert of Brandenberg, who had had to borrow a vast sum to give to the Pope before he would let him hold two bishoprics at once, and administer a third, when he was not canonically of age to hold even one. Albert was twenty-four. Luther may not have known of this arrangement and does not mention it; in any case he objected not to the way the money was used (and sometimes it was used wisely, the Wittenberg indulgences, for example, supporting the Castle Church and the university), but to the claim that indulgences effected reconciliation with God. Watch him, then, as at midday on All Saints' Eve, 1517, he walks with a friend to the Castle Church and affixes a notice to the door, where university teachers regularly posted their notices. But what Luther posted was an invitation to debate with him ninety-five theses or assertions on the "power and efficacy of Indulgences". No one took up the challenge. But, unknown to him, the ninety-five theses, which were in Latin, were translated into German and in a fortnight printed copies were circulating throughout Germany.

As yet Luther had no thought of breaking with Rome. In the matter of indulgences the Pope in fact corrected the worst abuses, and in a debate at Leipzig Luther's opponent, John Eck, allowed that their differences here could easily have been composed. But Luther had gone on to assert that the Roman Church had not always been above all other Churches, "at least not above the Greek". He had come to regard the papacy as a human institution. He was cited to appear at Rome to answer the charge of heresy. However, Frederick succeeded in getting the case transferred to Germany, where began a "tortuous series of negotiations culminating in Luther's hearing before the Diet of Worms".

During these years Luther succeeded by his writings in getting his views widely known and in winning a large following from among his countrymen. Then in the summer of 1520 the Pope issued a bull giving him sixty days to submit, and in the autumn his books were burned at Cologne and Mainz. His reply came on December 10th. Near the Elster Gate in Wittenberg a fire was kindled and into it were cast the volumes of the Canon Law and the Papal Decretals. Then Luther stepped forward and dropped into the flames the bull against himself. If we are to fix a date for Luther's break with Rome it is the winter of 1520–1.

By January the Pope had ready a bull of excommunication. But arrangements already begun still went forward for him to appear before the Diet or Council of the German nation which was to meet at Worms, on the Rhine, and over which the young Emperor Charles V would preside. Frederick procured for Luther a safe conduct and he appeared before the Diet in April. Great pressure was put on him to retract, but he refused: he would withdraw nothing he had written about the tyranny of the Pope. "Unless I am convicted by Scripture and plain reason . . . my conscience is captive to the Word of God. . . . To go against conscience is neither right nor safe. God help me. Amen." He had been given a safe conduct and he was allowed to go. Then (though not till May 26th) the Edict of Worms was signed. It declared Luther a convicted heretic, and said no one was to harbour him; his followers also were to be condemned and his books destroyed. Meanwhile Luther had been waylaid by a band of horsemen, instructed by Frederick, and taken for safety to Wartburg Castle.

He remained here for ten months and in three months translated the New Testament. The Old Testament in German followed later. During these months Melanchthon made a beginning at reform in Wittenberg by giving communion in both kinds. He was a moderate, and hoped longer than most that Reformers and Romanists might be reconciled, but the other Wittenberg leaders, Carlstadt and Zwilling, were extremists. Things began to happen. Priests married, monks and nuns left the cloister, meat was eaten on fast days, altars were overturned and images destroyed. Carlstadt rejected the worship of the saints, purgatory and prayers for the dead. "He was probably the first man in the sixteenth century to reach the conclusion that there ought to be neither dogma nor institution."[1] Of course there were disturbances. Then three lay "prophets" arrived from Zwickau who rejected infant baptism, said the Bible was unnecessary as the Holy Ghost spoke direct to men, and proclaimed the coming of the Kingdom through the slaughter of the ungodly. It was time for Luther to be invited back. He ran great risks; he was under the ban of Church and Empire, but he came.

SOME THINGS THAT LUTHER TAUGHT

1. First and foremost Luther taught the doctrine of Justification by Faith alone. Here his own experience was for him conclusive: the doors had opened to Paradise when he ceased to believe that he must propitiate an angry God by his good works. In the long and bitter controversy between Catholics and Reformers concerning this doctrine, each side misrepresented the other. The difference was really one of emphasis. Both Catholics and Reformers "asserted that man's salvation . . . was due to the work of Christ and the action of Divine Grace, and . . . implied an action of the human will in accepting the Divine gift and directing itself to good works".[2]

2. He taught the priesthood of all believers. Yet Luther held that a minister must be duly called, though it did not matter whether a bishop or another ordained him, since all who had been baptized were "priests without distinction". Lutheranism

[1] R. H. Murray: *Erasmus and Luther*, p. 177.
[2] Edwyn Bevan: *Christianity*, p. 167; and see pp. 165–8.

in fact came to exhibit considerable variety in the form of its ministry. In Sweden bishops whose own consecration was unimpeachable continued the succession, which remains to the present. In Finland it continued till less than a century ago. But in Denmark which early became Lutheran, superintendents were appointed, who adopted the title of bishop but did not receive episcopal consecration; and in Germany itself no attempt was made to maintain the Apostolic Succession. In Germany at first the civil ruler—"the godly prince"—exercised the authority which had been the bishop's.[1]

One way in which the laity exercised their priesthood was by hymn-singing. Luther himself wrote the words and music of many hymns (e.g. "God is a stronghold and a tower"). We should notice, too, the place which the home came to occupy in Lutheranism—and in Protestantism generally. The proper sphere for religion was the home not the monastery. At forty-two Luther married Katherine von Bora, who had been a nun, not because he was infatuated but to provide a home for her. There were six children whom he dearly loved, besides four orphans whom they brought up and student borders who helped them to make ends meet. The Elector made over the old Augustinian cloister for them to live in.[2]

3. Luther taught that pulpit takes precedence over altar—this came from a stress on the ministry of the Word.

4. That the only Sacraments are Baptism and the Lord's Supper, because they alone were instituted by Christ himself.

5. That the Lord's Supper is a thanksgiving and a communion but not a sacrifice.

6. That the Body and Blood of Christ are truly present and are given to the faithful in the Lord's Supper.

7. That communion should be in both kinds. (The custom of communicating the laity in one kind grew up in the later Middle Ages.)

8. That customs should be changed as little as need be though worship should be in the common tongue. Luther brought out his Mass in German in 1526. Vestments, lights, crucifix on the altar, genuflexions were in general retained, but variety was allowed in worship provided the essentials were kept.

[1] See *The Apostolic Ministry*, pp. 467–9.

[2] Bainton's *The Church of our Fathers*, pp. 146, 147, gives a letter, also printed in *Here I Stand*, which Luther wrote to four-year-old Hans: this is the Luther who wrote "Away in a manger" and a children's catechism.

9. Last, but very important, Luther taught that the civil ruler is head of the Church in his territory. It was only the civil ruler who could give the Church the protection and peace which it needed, and the Peasants' War (1524) had made Luther afraid of power in the hands of the people. But when, from fear of anarchy, he urged the State to "smite, stab and slay", and fifty thousand peasants perished, the Lutheran movement lost the support of the masses. In the south they remained Roman Catholic; for the rest the peasantry found a spiritual home in sects such as the Anabaptists.

LUTHERANISM TO THE RELIGIOUS PEACE OF AUGSBURG

This takes us beyond Luther's death in 1546. The names of two places, each of which enters the story twice, should be remembered.

(1) One is Speyer. Diets were held here in 1526 and 1529. At the time of the first, Philip of Hesse brought two hundred horsemen into the town. This Diet left every state free to act "as it would have to answer to God and the Emperor", and was followed by rapid Lutheran advance. The Diet of 1529, however, abandoned the principle adopted three years before. The Emperor's brother, Ferdinand of Austria, who presided, demanded the rooting out of heresy, and this Diet laid down that, in lands that had adopted the reform, Roman Catholics must be free to practise their religion, but Lutherans were not to be given a similar liberty in Roman Catholic territories. From the protest made by Philip of Hesse, John of Saxony, Frederick's successor, and other princes and by the representatives of thirteen imperial cities, came the name Protestant. (Neither party was ready to tolerate the other. Both believed that liberty of belief endangered the State, i.e. the conflict was becoming political. The remedy was emigration.)

(2) The other name is Augsburg. The Confession of Faith (the Augsburg Confession) read at a Diet held in 1530 became the doctrinal statement accepted by the entire Lutheran body. Melanchthon, who wrote it, meant it as an olive-branch. It was studiously moderate, stressing points held in common and slurring over differences. But it did not bring Catholics and Protestants together. Next year, under Philip of Hesse's leadership, the Schmalkald League of Protestants was formed for mutual protection, but it was many years before the Emperor struck. When he did in 1546, the league had grown weak and in 1547 Charles won an easy victory at Mühlberg. His attempt to

enforce religious uniformity was not very successful and in the end he found himself driven out of Germany. At another Diet, held in 1555, the Religious Peace of Augsburg was promulgated. This laid down the principle *Cuius regio, eius religio*, "Whose is the territory, his is the religion", thus recognizing the territorial principle and giving the Lutheran Church the same legal right to exist as Roman Catholicism. Unfortunately it legislated only for Lutheranism and Roman Catholicism. This left the Calvinists, the Reformed Church, not to mention the Anabaptists, outside the terms of the peace.

"*Picture Post*"

MARTIN LUTHER (1483–1546) AT ERFURT
From the picture by Noel Paton.   (See pages 151–6)

"Picture Post"

CALVIN (1509–64) AT THE COUNCIL OF GENEVA IN 1549.
From the picture by Labouchère. (See pages 166–9)

21

The Reformation Abroad: Zwingli— The Anabaptists—Calvin

THE DEBT OF THE REFORMATION MOVEMENT TO LUTHER

Outside Germany and the Scandinavian countries Calvin was to exert a greater influence on reform than Luther. Even though in most countries which separated from Rome the beginnings of reform were Lutheran, Calvinism (except in Germany and in Denmark and Sweden with their dependencies), was the type of doctrine that came to prevail. England is a special case, but in England also Calvinism exerted more influence than Lutheranism. Did we then give too much attention to Luther? No. "There was something about this big, imperfect man," as Edwyn Bevan has said, "of such a kind that what he felt shook the hearts of thousands in Europe, broke up the crust of things, and changed the face of the world."[1] To quote T. M. Lindsay: "To the common people in every land in Europe up till about 1540, when Calvin's individuality began to make itself felt, Luther represented the Reformation."[2] It was twenty years before the Reformation came to mean also, and in the end to mean rather, Calvin. Calvin was twenty-six years younger than Luther.

ZWINGLI AND THE SWISS REFORMATION

Ulrich Zwingli (1484–1531) was not a comparable figure with either Luther or Calvin. He was Luther's contemporary, less than two months younger, and he openly broke with the papacy not long after Luther—in 1522. Zwingli belonged to German-speaking Switzerland. He was born in an Alpine village where his father was magistrate: he had uncles who were priests. He studied at the universities of Vienna and Basle, and like Luther was an accomplished musician. At Glarus, where he was

[1] Edwyn Bevan, *Christianity*, p. 170.
[2] T. M. Lindsay, *History of the Reformation*, vol. ii, p. 16.

village priest from 1506, he saw the harm done by the long-established custom by which the Swiss provided infantry for the papal wars. He went to Italy twice as chaplain with his village contingent and was present at two battles. Then he was a priest at Einsiedeln, a famous pilgrimage centre, where the abbey possessed a winking Madonna, and here he came up

Paul Popper

ULRICH ZWINGLI (1484–1531)
SWISS REFORMER

against trickery and credulity. He was a first-rate scholar and, when Erasmus's Greek New Testament came out in 1516, he copied out the whole of St Paul's Epistles. That was before he became a priest at the minster at Zurich, in 1519. (The best side of the Reformation was a return to the Bible.)

Soon after coming to Zurich he denounced indulgences, but whereas Luther had done so because they endangered people's souls, Zwingli did so because to him they were just foolishness. That is the difference between the two men. The Reformation soon reached beyond Zurich and before Zwingli died, all German-speaking Switzerland, apart from Lucerne and the Forest cantons, had embraced the reform—at any rate officially. Zwingli was slain fighting at the battle of Cappell in 1531, when the Romanist Forest cantons invaded Zurich: Luther considered his death a judgement; a minister should not take up arms. Two years before this Zwinglians had joined with Lutherans in the protest at Speyer from which the name Protestant derives; but Luther always distrusted Zwingli. The "middle way", which was Luther's, never at any time attracted Zwingli, and whereas Luther allowed practices to continue so long as Scripture did not forbid them, Zwingli would allow nothing that Scripture did not command. Lutherans kept their organs, but Zwingli, fine musician though he was, allowed no instrumental music in worship. In that respect he was like Calvin (who disliked even the singing of psalms) and, as we have already seen, like the Eastern Orthodox Church.

VIEWS OF THE HOLY COMMUNION

In his teaching about the Eucharist Luther explicitly affirmed the Real Presence and held a view which is technically known as consubstantiation. This asserts that in the Holy Communion the substance of the Body and Blood of Christ is added to the substance of the bread and wine. The Roman, medieval but not primitive, theory of transubstantiation asserts that the change wrought at consecration converts the substance of the material bread and wine into that of Christ's Body and Blood: the "accidents" (i.e. what you can touch or taste), remain, but what we may call the "breadness" and the "wineness" have disappeared and been replaced by our Lord's Body and Blood. This view, whatever there is to be said against it, is in fact a spiritual interpretation of the Real Presence, but it is none the less certain that it was often made to appear grossly materialistic. Zwingli's reaction was to say that the Sacrament is a bare sign. The bread and the wine are only a reminder of the salvation won for us on Calvary. "This is my Body" means "This signifies my Body" and how he meant this to be taken Zwingli explains. It is the same as if a wife showed a ring engraved with her husband's portrait and said, "Look, this is my husband". The bread and the wine are signs which represent what is absent. The service does us good because it reminds us, and by our sharing in it we remind each other, of our redemption by Christ, and so our faith is strengthened; and Christ of course will be present in the manner in which He is always present "where two or three are gathered together"—but His presence is independent of the sacramental signs and unrelated to them. With Calvin this is not so. To Calvin the bread and the wine are signs which exhibit what is present.[1] Calvin even speaks of a Real Presence and says that the *substance* of Christ's Body and Blood is "truly given unto us". By this he means, however, *His power and virtue*, and his view came to be known as virtualism. This is nearer to Luther's view than receptionism, which maintains that there is no change whatever in the elements but "Christ is eaten with the heart". Both lie between the extremes of transubstantiation and Zwingli's bare sign, the technical name for which is sacramentarianism.

The Reformers, in their teaching about the Eucharist, laid stress on the necessity of faith. But on any view which regards the Sacrament as a channel of grace, faith is required if the worshipper is to benefit, and the wicked by partaking incur judgement rather than life (cf. 1 Cor. 11. 27–30). Throughout the Middle Ages the aspect of the Eucharist as a communion had been in the background. The Mass had been regarded almost exclusively as a sacrifice, an actual repetition of Christ's sacrifice on Calvary—a doctrine which conflicted with the sufficiency of Christ's sacrifice on the Cross. In reaction against this medieval and late conception of the eucharistic sacrifice, the continental Reformers thought of it not as a sacrifice at all, but only as a thanksgiving and communion. The first English Reformers probably agreed with them. The Prayer Book, however, does not deny the sacrificial aspect of the Eucharist, but only the sense in which it was "commonly said" to be one.[2]

THE ANABAPTISTS

The Anabaptists have already been noticed in connexion with the aftermath of the Peasants' War. The name means "over-again-baptizers" and was what their enemies called them; they called themselves Baptists. They had, of course, been baptized as infants, as was everybody in medieval Europe, except the

[1] See Lindsay, *op. cit.*, p. 59, and cf. Dix: *The Shape of the Liturgy*, p. 633.
[2] See Article XXXI.

Jews living in their ghettos. But infant baptism the Anabaptists held to be useless. The Bible did not say "Baptize *infants*" and infants could not have the requisite faith. (The Reformers generally held that in their case the faith of the sponsors sufficed.) To the Anabaptists the "believer" was a person baptized after conversion. The sect seems to have had its roots in communities of pious, lowly folk which existed, despite authority, in medieval Europe, as did the Lollards in England. A constant note in the Anabaptist teaching is a sympathy with the down-trodden masses. Their services were simple, and what principally distinguished them, apart from the custom of believers' baptism, which did not go back behind the Reformation, was their insistence that the Church should be completely separate from the State and absolutely free from all civil control. Their ideal was a "gathered Church" of believers only—and since no one was baptized without being warned that martyrdom was probably in store for him or her, their standard of life remained at a high level. Here and there, and very occasionally, there were excesses, and, in view of the terrible persecutions which they endured, this is not to be wondered at; but on the whole they were quiet folk who had no thought of injuring the State. What made them suspect to nearly everyone was their view that the Church should only embrace some of the inhabitants of the State, since all could not be expected to reach the standard required. This was revolutionary.

Zwingli, "aghast to see the medieval unity shattered", as early as 1525 invoked the intervention of the State in Zurich. Anabaptists were fiercely persecuted both by Roman Catholics and Protestants; Protestants putting them to death as a rule by drowning, and Romanists by burning or roasting them near a fire! Their courage was amazing, and Philip of Hesse said he saw more improvement of life among them than among Lutherans. Luther was at first distressed at the persecution. "It is not right," he said, "and I am deeply troubled that the poor people are so pitifully put to death, burned and cruelly slain." He acquiesced when he thought them seditious. If they were not seditious they should be banished—which was Philip of Hesse's opinion as well. In any case, they suffered terribly, and yet the movement grew, spreading across Germany and into the Low Countries and Italy and even into eastern England, where Anabaptists were burned by Cranmer. All modern Baptist churches originate from this movement. The Baptist Church in England came through Amsterdam where John Smyth, a Cambridge

Puritan, who had been preacher to the City of Lincoln, had himself and some fellow exiles rebaptized by the Memnonite (i.e. Anabaptist) church there. But that was not until early in the next century.

CALVIN (1509–64) AND THE REFORMATION IN GENEVA

To come back to Calvin. John Calvin (Jean Chauvin) was a Frenchman, born in Picardy, the son of a lawyer with a good practice. John shared the education of the children of a noble family which he entered, his father paying his expenses. He always remained the cultured and polished French gentleman, whereas Luther, the peasant's son, remained rough and rather boorish although he became a university professor. At fourteen Calvin went with the three sons of the de Montmor family to continue their education in Paris. His father, who as a lawyer knew some of the higher clergy, was able to obtain for him more than one church benefice (substitutes doing the duty), and in this way paid for his education at Paris. He became one of the best scholars of the age. At twenty-five he resigned his benefices; he had either to resign them then or be ordained. He studied law in Orleans. Then we find him a member of a reforming group in Poitiers, acting as minister and giving Holy Communion.

Calvin was never ordained. Probably he thought of himself as an evangelist, not as a member of the ordinary ministry. Just as the Apostles belonged to the extraordinary ministry so from time to time God, he said, raised up evangelists in the Apostles' stead, "as has been done in our time". He was very unlike Luther. As Canon Maynard Smith has said: "Luther was emotional, sometimes boisterous, often in the highest spirits and often in the depths of depression, never happy when he was alone. He loved music, beer, talk and good fellowship . . . Calvin was cold, self-disciplined and intense; he cared nothing for the arts or pleasures of life. . . . He had very few friends." But they had their points in common. "Both men were absolutely sincere and zealous for what they believed was the truth. . . . Both based their religion entirely on the Bible." They both believed in justification by faith alone and in pre-destination,[1] "so that the salvation of some was due to the

---

[1] I.e. the belief that God has appointed some of mankind to eternal life and (the reformers would have added) some to perdition. It went back through St Augustine to St Paul. It is arguable that St Paul did not commit himself to the doctrine of predestination to damnation.

arbitrary caprice of God, but Calvin emphasized his belief that the majority of men had been created for eternal torture, for he saw that few came up to his standard of righteousness, and that righteousness he regarded as a sign of God's election."[1]

Calvin believed that only what was in the Bible was allowable and he claimed that the presbyterian system which he set out in Book IV of the *Institutes of the Christian Religion*, written when he was twenty-seven (just before he came to Geneva), was Biblical. At the head of each church should be a bishop, presbyter or pastor (offices which he regarded as identical) and associated with him should be lay elders and deacons. The deacons had charge of the sick and poor; the elders were "seniors selected from the people to unite with the bishop in pronouncing censures and exercising discipline." The exercise of discipline he regarded as fundamental and he was banished for three years (1538–41) from Geneva by the city council because he would not allow all and sundry to communicate. He went to Strassburg, where he married, and ministered to a French congregation.

We should notice the stress which Calvin laid on communion. He knew that a weekly communion was the primitive rule and ought to be revived, but a quarterly communion was the most that could be established at the time. We have to remember that, under the system which Calvin set up, the faithful *had* to communicate on Sacrament Sundays (except the excommunicate). They had no choice in the matter any more than they were at liberty to go to church on Sunday or not as they felt inclined, or even to omit hearing the weekday sermons.

The city council were glad to get Calvin back on his own terms; yet he never succeeded in setting up in Geneva a church that was master in its own house such as John Knox established in Scotland. In Geneva pastors, elders and deacons were all chosen by the city council, though in the case of pastors the church had a right of veto through its Consistory or legislative council composed of all the pastors and elders. The council always chose the elders from among its own members, which meant that the elders were also magistrates.

Calvin came to Geneva, which had the year before adopted the Reform, intending to spend only one night there. Then an older French reformer, William Farel, finding that he was there, got him, not without difficulty, to stay on and help him,

[1] *Church Quarterly Review*, July–September 1940, art., "The Reformation at Home and Abroad".

instead of devoting his life to the pursuit of learning and the writing of books as he had meant to do. In twenty-three years he turned an immoral, pleasure-loving city into one where almost no amusement of any sort was permitted. Dancing, songs, novels were all prohibited; all sports except archery were frowned upon and card-playing was condemned utterly. Men and women alike had to wear sober garments, and women might not braid their hair. "Every household lived its life under the supervision of a spiritual police." What is noticeable is not so much the number of prosecutions; there are probably places to-day where as high a proportion of the population appears in the Magistrates' Courts; but that no difference was made between a sin and a crime punishable by law, and also that the sentences were most severe. A child was beheaded for striking its parents. Torture was resorted to in order to get confessions out of people; and in the four years 1542 to 1546, fifty-eight heretics were put to death.

Some of Geneva's citizens no doubt found their new yoke heavy, but to many of the Protestants in other countries Geneva seemed the ideal Christian city. Refugees flocked there from France and Italy, from England and Scotland, to learn of Calvin, until they numbered as many as six thousand, nearly half the native population. What attracted them? Was it that Calvinism, though not the "left wing" of the Protestant movement, was as certainly not a "middle way"? Or was it the attempt, which Professor Tawney says was characteristic of Geneva for something like half a century, to make the law of God prevail over the whole of life—business life as well as personal life? The control of prices, of rates of interest and so on, seems to us very modern, but it was after all only in line with the Church's emphasis in the Middle Ages on the "just price". What in fact happened in Geneva, and elsewhere where men devoted their lives to business and not to pleasure, was that they became wealthy, and then went on to believe that they were for this reason acceptable to God. To be poor meant that you must be wicked, and that it would be an affront to God to help you!

Luther never distrusted Calvin as he did Zwingli, and unlike Zwingli, Calvin was able to sign the Augsburg Confession, his views according nearly enough with those of the Lutherans. But just as he was himself more austere by temperament than Luther, so the worship of the Reformed, or Presbyterian Church, was bare and shorn of ceremonial to an extent unknown in

Lutheranism. It made inroads, however, into the south of Germany, and the older Zwinglian churches there and in Switzerland, adopted Calvinism and ceased to have an independent history. To the French Huguenots,[1] whose Church grew up amid bitter persecution, and many of whose early leaders were trained in Geneva by Calvin himself, Calvinism seemed *the religion* to the exclusion of any other form of Christianity.

We ought to notice France not only because of the massacre of St Bartholomew's Day (1572) and the thirty years of anarchy and religious strife which it experienced in the sixteenth century, but because the Edict of Nantes in 1598 which ended them accorded a degree of religious freedom which had no parallel elsewhere at that time. Huguenots were allowed the public exercise of their religion wherever it had become established during the two preceding years, with the exception of Paris itself; and even there courtiers might worship according to the Reformed faith behind closed doors. Although behind the Edict there was an ulterior motive, to win back by clemency to the Catholic fold those whom force had failed to win, French Calvinists were for a time safe. The Churches of Holland and of Scotland also looked to Geneva for their model, and the Presbyterian Church of Scotland shows Presbyterianism as Calvin meant it to be much more truly than does the Church in Geneva. In Scotland appointments were really made by the people as a whole; the system became nation-wide, with its Kirk Sessions, its Synod and General Assembly; and there too Calvinism "ruled the people with a rod of iron and without compromise".[2]

---

[1] At first a nickname, perhaps taken from a person named "Hugues", which was given by the Roman Catholics to the Protestants of France, and then used by them as a badge of honour.

[2] K. D. Mackenzie in *The Apostolic Ministry*, p. 472.

22

The Reformation at Home:
Henry VIII

THE POLITICAL FOREGROUND

Would a Reformation without a break with Rome, such as had already occurred in some measure in Spain, have been possible in England? The kind of Reformation which John Colet, Dean of St Paul's, Sir Thomas More, and their friend Erasmus (who was often in England before 1515), all of them men of the New Learning,[1] sought to procure was a general reform of the Western Church. Colet died in 1519, before Luther's break with Rome. Erasmus, anxious though he was for reform, as we have seen, deplored Luther's action. He died at Basle, in 1536, in communion with Rome. In the previous summer More died on the scaffold saying "that he was the King's good servant, but God's first". By then Henry had, for political reasons, brought about the break. Unlike the Reformation abroad, the English Reformation did not begin with religion and go on to affect politics and economics. It began with politics; it was mixed up from the first with economics (with the King's need of money, which the English Parliament, always in those days niggardly, refused to raise by taxation), and there were social causes (the Church was much too powerful and owned much too large a share of the nation's land), but it could not have happened if religion had not also come in.

Things might have worked out differently had the papacy been different and had Henry been different; but the course which events took was due to Henry and his desire to dominate the Church and reduce it to subservience for his own ends. In 1527 he had been married for eighteen years, and he had no

[1] Oxford, shortly before More became a student there early in the last decade of the fifteenth century, had welcomed the New Learning. A visiting Italian first taught Greek, but More was able to study under Grocyn and Linacre, who had returned from Italy imbued with the spirit of the Renaissance. Not only was Linacre a Greek scholar but he founded the Royal College of Physicians in London in 1518.

heir. Was it true that his marriage to Catherine of Aragon had never been a marriage at all? Catherine had been his brother Arthur's wife for five months. Had the papal dispensation been wrongly obtained? An heir he must have, and he was at the time passionately in love with Anne Boleyne. He must have his marriage with Catherine declared null and void. He does not seem to have imagined that the Pope would make difficulties; and in fact Wolsey assured him of success. He did not question the Pope's authority—until he could not get what he wanted.

The Pope, Clement VII, shuffled. "The King's great matter" (as the divorce, more properly the nullity of the marriage, was called) had no sooner been broached than Rome was sacked by the troops of the Emperor Charles V because the papacy had made an alliance with France, and Clement was reduced to submission. Clement dared not offend Charles, who was Catherine's nephew. He was indeed a past master in the art of delaying, but in 1529 he granted a commission for the case to be tried by Cardinals Wolsey and Campeggio in England, giving the Italian cardinal instructions, unknown to Wolsey, not to give judgement until further orders. On June 23rd, when sentence was due to be pronounced Campeggio adjourned the court till October, by which time the case had been recalled to Rome. Wolsey's fall followed; he had been unable to get "the King's great matter" brought to a successful conclusion.

It was now that the Parliament known to history as the Reformation Parliament was elected. It sat till 1536. Yet it is unlikely that Henry as yet contemplated the breach with Rome. For some time longer he tried to get his way *without seeking [a] remedy elsewhere* as a petition, sent to the Pope, and signed by leading men of the realm, put it. Many of the universities of Europe had given an opinion favourable to Henry and this had already been conveyed to the Pope. The petition was meant to back this up. But it was clear that the Pope would not declare the marriage null. The King had to find another way; which meant that the Church at home must be brought to heel. In 1531 the whole body of the clergy was charged with a breach of Praemunire, for having recognized Wolsey as legate.[1] It was

[1] The acts of Praemunire (1353 and 1365) outlawed those who pleaded at Rome matters which the royal courts could decide, i.e. they made it an offence to assert the authority and jurisdiction of the Pope in England. *Praemunire*, from Latin *praemonēre*, "to warn", is the opening word of the Latin writ summoning a person to answer such a charge.

as grotesque as the charge against Wolsey that he had acted as legate (i.e. for a foreign power). Henry himself, for his own purposes, had got Wolsey made legate and the clergy had detested Wolsey's arrogance and interference. But they only obtained pardon by paying in the two Convocations a fine of nearly £120,000—then a very large sum indeed—and by acknowledging the King as supreme Head of the Church and clergy of England "as far as the law of Christ allows." The Convocations of Canterbury and York managed to get the latter phrase inserted. Next year came the submission of the clergy, who were forced to give up their right to legislate in Church matters in their own Convocations independently of Parliament.

But now, with the death of Archbishop Warham (the submission had broken his heart), came Henry's opportunity to get an archbishop who firmly believed in the royal authority even over the Church, and was prepared to defy the Pope. Thomas Cranmer's views were known; he was chosen, the Pope being induced to issue the necessary bulls for his appointment (1533). We need not doubt Cranmer when he said that he came to the office unwillingly. But he believed the marriage with Catherine was null and void and on May 23rd pronounced it such. This was followed by a decree pronouncing valid Henry's secret marriage with Anne in the previous January. The Pope replied by censuring Henry but for a time held the censure in suspense; then in November the papal excommunication was published in Dunkirk. Parliament also acted. It brought into operation an act, already passed but held in suspense, transferring the payment of annates from the Pope to the King, and passed acts abolishing Peter's Pence, and forbidding appeals to Rome. It also embodied in Acts of Parliament the submission of the clergy and the royal supremacy, leaving out the phrase "as far as the law of Christ allows". The break with Rome was complete.

THE RELIGIOUS BACKGROUND

Henry's divorce was not popular. How was it, then, that he was able to get Parliament and the Convocations to carry through the breach with Rome, when even at the end of his reign the doctrinal Reformation had touched at most a quarter of the people and those mostly in London, Kent and Essex? The answer is partly fear. There is a second reason. In the sixteenth century people had an exaggerated deference to kingship, which made them unwilling to criticize whatever actions a king might take. But most of all it was owing to the almost universal dislike of the papacy. Even most of the clergy disliked Rome. Opposition to Henry was almost non-existent, and such as there was was stamped out. The Nun of Kent, Elizabeth Barton, who prophesied that dreadful things would happen to Henry, was hanged with her supporters. More and the saintly Fisher, Bishop of Rochester, went to the block for refusing to assent to the act of 1535 which settled the succession on Henry's children by Anne. From the Tower More watched the three Charterhouse priors "as cheerfully going to their deaths as bridegrooms to their marriage"; they were dragged through the streets to Tyburn bound on hurdles. Otherwise there was practically no opposition till the rebellion known as the Pilgrimage of Grace (1536).

There were, of course, some who welcomed the change on religious grounds. Some were early attracted by the teachings of Luther. As early as 1518 a little group of young Cambridge dons began meeting at the White Horse Tavern to discuss the new ideas. The meetings went on for some ten years, and the members included Tyndale, Latimer, Ridley, and Parker, Elizabeth's archbishop. Despite Wolsey's prohibition, Lutheran books were smuggled in. With our very extensive trade with the Low Countries and Germany nothing like an "iron curtain" was possible.

There was never much heresy in England. One movement deriving in the main from Wiclif and his poor priests or preachers [1] lived on underground and provided every now and then a few martyrs. The strongholds of the Lollards were London and East Anglia, and parts of the East Midlands, and here Lutheran influences were earliest felt. Lollardy had no very fixed body of beliefs and its followers were not people of importance. They maintained an outward conformity, but they resented the power and privileges of the clergy, and even more they disliked the monastic houses. Lollardy has been well described by Professor Whitney as "a kind of lowly discontent", but it had a literature of its own, tracts written for the unlearned, and it had the Wiclifite translation of the Bible. This, or such parts of it as could be got, was read and treasured in Lollard households. A good many manuscripts survive, nearly all written after 1408, when

---

[1] After Wiclif's death they were laymen, whose sympathy with the peasantry gave them leanings towards communism. Wiclif denied transsubstantiation, basing his objection on philosophic grounds, but believed in the Real Presence of Christ in the sacrament.

the Wiclif Bible was prohibited. The fact that there existed in England at the time of the Reformation a stronger feeling against vernacular translations of the Bible than in any other country, is due to Wiclif's version being the Lollard Bible. Lollards and Lutherans were not much alike, the former being humble folk filled with a "discontent" that had existed for generations, the latter being either young university dons (some of them friars), or merchants who had contacts with Germany; but the two groups could and did combine to defy the Pope and welcome the curtailment of the excessive power and influence of the clergy. Particularly if they were of the laity, they welcomed a restraining hand on the Church's right to interfere in their daily lives.

Townsmen, particularly the merchant classes, had for some three hundred years combined devotion with anticlericalism. They disliked the Church's having things so much its own way. They were still devout, lavishing care and money on the churches, but they were ill-instructed, and a ready prey for new ideas that might be abroad, particularly if the new ideas savoured of anticlericalism. Couple all this with England's need of a strong ruler, and it is not so remarkable that Henry "got away with" substituting himself for the Pope as supreme head of the Church of his realm.

Perhaps not quite that. Henry never claimed a right to ordain or minister the sacraments. What Henry asserted was his complete control over the Church of his realm, which he found it useful to exercise in the main through Parliament. He did not claim to be the founder of a new Church. In fact the contrary, for having decreed that the Bishop of Rome had no authority in this realm of England, he went on to seek "in sundry old and authentic histories" for proof that his decree only restored what once had been. This was far-fetched, but English kings had stood up to the Pope of their days. The Church of England has always claimed to be the old Catholic Church of this land —now Catholic and Reformed—but not a new Church.

THE DISSOLUTION OF THE MONASTERIES

The Supremacy Act made Henry visitor of the monastic houses. In 1535 he appointed Thomas Cromwell, a layman and a lawyer, as his Vicar-General to carry out a visitation of monasteries and convents. Edward III and Henry V had suppressed alien priories (i.e. priories belonging to monasteries abroad), and Wolsey suppressed thirty religious houses to found Cardinal College (now Christ Church) Oxford, and Ipswich School. This showed Henry the way. He, through his Vicar-General, suppressed something like six hundred. There is no doubt there were too many monasteries, and some could usefully have been dissolved. "When endowments are in excess of needs, a Supreme Head ought to direct them into other channels. The principle is sound; Henry's application of it was wrong. The channel into which he diverted the wealth of the Church was his own pocket."[1] His Vicar-General also did pretty well out of the dissolution; he had Church jewels worth many thousands of pounds in his London home when he was arrested five years later. So did the new governing class who bought the monastic lands; Henry did not give them away as a rule. These they proceeded to let out or sell to others, so that soon a lot of people came to have a vested interest in the new order.

The suppression was in two stages. The smaller houses which were adjudged to be morally scandalous (this is more than doubtful, except in a few cases, though they may have been lax) were dissolved by act of Parliament (1536). The larger houses were encouraged to surrender themselves on the score of their shortcomings, though Parliament itself had declared that religion was well kept in them. Parliament gave no authority for the suppression of the greater houses, but once they had been suppressed it confirmed the King's possession of their property. The abbots of Glastonbury, Reading and Colchester, who would not surrender their houses, were hanged on such charges as having hidden the Church property; so was the abbot of Woburn, who, despite having taken the supremacy oath, had said that "the Bishop of Rome's authority was good and lawful." The nunneries gave themselves up without trouble. There were many fewer of them and their suppression had the least social effect. But the monks were not turned adrift penniless; some five thousand were given pensions. Friars received nothing. If a pensioner subsequently received preferment, as many did, the pension stopped. Many abbots and priors became bishops or deans. Nuns too received a small pension. There were not more than fifteen hundred of them. Some of them married; others lived together, keeping their rule so far as they could.

It was the dissolution of the smaller religious houses that occasioned the Pilgrimage of Grace. By now it was clear that the royal supremacy meant plunder and loot; and in the north,

[1] H. Maynard Smith: *Henry VIII and the Reformation*, pp. 108, 109.

absentee landlords, poverty and unemployment. When the revolt was over, nearly two hundred persons were sent to their deaths. With the dissolution of the monasteries went, too, the destruction of shrines, such as that of Thomas Becket at Canterbury. The wealth of the shrine of St Thomas was conveyed to London in twenty-six carts. Nothing Henry did was more popular than his execution in 1540 of his Vicar-General, Thomas Cromwell, who had carried through all this spoliation.

What was the effect of the suppression of the religious orders on the social life of the time? In trying to adjudge this we must remember that the laity had been concerned for centuries as stewards, bailiffs, auditors and in other capacities, with the affairs of the monasteries, much of whose land was leased to laymen. This made the transition to the new order much easier. The country gentry who had helped to manage the properties "as often as not succeeded in buying them. The percentage of arable land was high, and the lay element which had served the monastic establishment would, on the whole, not find much difficulty in finding employment. . . . The distress must have varied greatly in different parts of the country, in some places hardly noticeable, severe in others—especially in the lonely places where the hospitality of the monks was a real boon to travellers and monastic ministrations to the poor were their only alleviation."[1]

THE SIX ARTICLES

In 1540, however, a halt was being called to the changes. By the middle of the previous decade, translations of the Bible in English had been permitted and in 1538 an injunction ordered the setting up in all churches, "on this side the feast of Easter next coming", of "one book of the whole Bible in the largest volume, in English". Another injunction issued at the same time ordered the keeping in every parish of "one book or register" in which all baptisms, marriages and burials were to be recorded. Although many parishes seemingly did not begin to keep registers till well on in the reign of Elizabeth, the parish registers for the next two or three centuries furnish so many sidelights on the life and customs of the times, being often far more than a mere record of those "wedded, christened or buried", that their first introduction should not pass unnoticed. But to go back to the Bible, now set up in churches in the English tongue, in 1543 Parliament issued restrictions on its being read;

[1] F. M. Powicke: *The Reformation in England*, pp. 22, 23.

and as we shall see in the opening chapter of the next volume, labourers and the like and all women except gentlewomen were forbidden to read it. The Church services, still in Latin, had been too much interrupted by people reading the Bible aloud.

Englishmen, as Sir Maurice Powicke says, were in general "ready to do without the Pope, but were prepared for nothing else". As the old services were kept, to the content of most, so to a large extent was the old theology. The Six Articles Statute makes this clear. Not merely the Real Presence but transubstantiation is insisted upon—to deny it became punishable by burning and the confiscation of one's goods to the State. To maintain that communion must be in both kinds, that the clergy might marry, that vows of chastity need not be observed, that private masses should not continue, and that auricular confession was not necessary, all were made punishable by death, though, except for the denial of transubstantiation, imprisonment might be substituted if the opinion were given up. The bishops did not want the act. It was essentially a lay measure and it was the laity who wished to enforce its penalties, but Henry was content to terrorize the people with this "whip with the six strings" and to pick his victims.

What, however, were his own private thoughts about religion and the changes he had made? A year before he died he lectured the Commons on the subject of religion. He said: "Of this I am sure, that charity was never so faint amongst you, virtuous and godly living was never less used, nor God himself amongst Christians was never less reverenced, honoured, or served." It has been held that here we have Henry's "own final condemnation of his own policy."[1]

The death of Henry VIII on January 28, 1547, brings to a close the first phase of the Reformation in England. The Lutherans, who always distrusted him, were wont to say that the "gospel of Harry" was his own private gain. In any case it is not right to identify the attitude to religion of one who has been described, not unjustly, as "no Protestant, but a wicked Catholic king",[2] with that of the English reformers generally. Already changes were on their way which would affect profoundly English life and thought in the succeeding centuries. The Bible had appeared, with official sanction, in an English dress, as had one liturgical service, the English Litany, which by royal injunction superseded the Latin processionals in the

[1] R. W. Chambers: *Thomas More*, p. 384.
[2] H. L. Goudge: *The Church of England and Reunion*, p. 24.

summer of 1544. We were to become very soon a people whose whole outlook on life as well as whose habits of devotion would be moulded by the Bible and in only slightly lesser degree by the Book of Common Prayer. It is with these matters that the second and concluding volume, which will carry the story of the Christian Church down to the present day, will be first concerned.

Appendix

CLASS EXERCISES AND ACTIVITIES (Vol. I)

Messrs George Philip and Son, Ltd., 32, Fleet Street, London, E.C.4, publish outline maps which can be used with these Exercises. The teacher should get a catalogue. Useful maps are:

England and Wales (coastline only), Imperial Quarto 3*d.*,
    Crown Quarto 2*d.*
Scotland, Imperial Quarto 3*d.*
Ireland, Imperial Quarto 3*d.*
Europe, Imperial Quarto 3*d.*, Crown Quarto 2*d.*
Asia, Imperial Quarto 3*d.*, Crown Quarto 2*d.*
Turkey, Syria and Iraq, Crown Quarto 2*d.*
South-Western Asia and Valley of Nile, Imperial Quarto 3*d.*

Map-building sheets for the teacher's use (44 by 34 inches) are also published, 4*s.* each map, eyeletted. Details can be added in chalk and removed with a duster. (More expensive editions, mounted on wooden ledges, 8*s.*, on cloth and rollers, 16*s.* 6*d.*)

Chapter 1

1. From St Paul's Epistles make a list of some of the Churches which he founded.

2. Mark in on an outline map the main centres of Christianity around the Mediterranean at the end of the Apostolic age.

3. Discover from Romans 16 the names of some of the Christians at Rome. (The Epistle was sent by St Paul to Rome before he had himself been there.) Look up the cross-references in the case of Priscilla (Prisca) and Aquila and Rufus.

Chapter 2

1. Suppose you have been converted by listening to a Christian preacher in the market-place. Write a letter telling a friend all about it and what happened afterwards.

2. Describe the rite of Christian initiation in Hippolytus's day. Is such a rite ever practised in churches of the Anglican communion at the present day?

3. Look up carefully the references in the section on "Instruction". (For further information about the Common Teaching see P. Carrington, *The Primitive Christian Catechism* (S.P.C.K.) or E. G. Selwyn, *I Peter*, Essay 2.)

179

Chapter 3

1. Describe a Sunday morning service during the days of persecution. Take either worship in the catacombs or in a private house.

2. What can we learn from the Acts of the Apostles about the Christian ministry?

Chapter 4

1. St John the Divine was exiled to Patmos under Domitian. Examine the following passages: Rev. 2. 13; 6. 9; 12. 11; 17. 6; 20. 4. Why does the attitude towards the civil power differ so markedly from that of St Paul (cf. Rom. 13. 1–7) and St Peter (cf. 1 Pet. 2. 13, 14)? (Note that at Pergamum there was a temple dedicated to Augustus and Rome which was the centre of Emperor-worship for that part of Asia; and that before Nero such persecution as the Church had experienced was sporadic and from the Jews.)

2. Write an eye-witness account of Nero's mad garden-parties.

Chapter 5

1. Draw a plan of a Roman basilica.

2. Mark out with stakes on a grass plot the ground-plan of the Roman-British church at Silchester. The measurements are given in the chapter. The church should be made to face west if this is possible. Owing to the impossibility of indicating the thickness of the walls, the building will look larger than it was, but even so its smallness will be apparent.

3. What benefits did Constantine's conversion confer on the Church? Make a list of the most important of these.

Chapter 6

1. Describe the monks of Egypt; or, write a short account of St Antony.

2. Read the description of an Egyptian "laura" or lane of cells i.e. a monastic settlement, in the desert in the first chapter of Kingsley's *Hypatia*.

3. Discuss the purpose of religious communities. Reference might be made to the saying *Orare est laborare*, "to pray is to work", and *Laborare est orare*, "to work is to pray."

Chapter 7

1. Read the first and second sequences of Scene 2 of Miss Dorothy Sayers' play-sequence, *The Man Born to be King*. Note carefully the expressions used by the Three Kings.

2. Discuss whether the recitation of a Creed should be regarded solely as a statement of belief. Can it be regarded also as an act of personal allegiance?

3. Compare the Apostles' and the Nicene Creeds and discover how much they have in common.

Appendix

Chapter 8

1. Copy the Lord's Prayer in Gothic.
2. Read chapter 4 of Mr. H. V. Morton's *Through Lands of the Bible*. Note the pictures of the Coptic altar and of the Korban breads.
3. Mark in on an outline map of Asia the centres of Christianity in the Middle and Far East mentioned in this chapter. (See endpapers, Latourette, HEC, ii.)

Chapter 9

1. Write an essay describing some of the main features of Islam.
2. Christian missions have not often been effective in the conversion of Moslems. Can you think of any reasons to account for this?
3. "Islam is still the strongest foe of Christianity." Is this statement, made in the nineteen-thirties, true to-day? Do you think that both Christianity and Islam are menaced by a godless materialism?

Chapter 10

1. Mark in on outline maps of Ireland and Scotland, some of the places associated with St Ninian, St Patrick and St Columba.
2. Give reasons why the missions noticed in this chapter met with such great success.
3. Discuss the place which a community like that at Iona could play in the life of the Church to-day.

Chapter 11

1. Find out all you can about St Gregory and St Augustine of Canterbury. Then sketch a series of short scenes, beginning with St Gregory and the English boys in the slave-market at Rome, and ending with King Edwin's baptism at York. (Materials should be readily available. See Bede, *Eccles. Hist.*, bk. 1, chs. 23–26, and—for St Gregory and the boys—bk. 2, ch. 1, last section; for Paulinus and Edwin, bk. 2, chs. 9, 13 and 14. In some schools impromptu acting might be attempted.)
2. Write an account of the Sutton Hoo ship-burial.
3. Are there any place-names in your locality which suggest the kind of association mentioned in this chapter.

Chapter 12

1. Read the story of Caedmon in Bede.
2. Mark in place-names on an outline map.

Chapter 13

1. Mark in on an outline map some of the places in Europe which were affected by the English mission. (The map in Stenton, *Anglo-Saxon England*, p. 164, should be consulted.)

2. Describe the life-work of either St Boniface or King Alfred.

3. Copy the Lord's Prayer from the West Saxon Gospels.

4. Visit, if possible, a church with some surviving pre-Conquest work.

Chapter 14

1. Write a description either of St Sophia or of an Eastern Orthodox service.

2. Consider the question of division within the Body of Christ. Why must schism be harmful, and to whom is it harmful?

3. What special qualities do you think a Church in bondage would develop? Discuss.

Chapter 15

1. What is the meaning of the City of God in the Bible? Consider the following passages: Psalm 48; Heb. 12. 22 and 13. 14; Rev. 3. 12 and 21 *passim*. Is or is not the view of St Gregory the Great that "Holy Church is the City of the Lord" in agreement with these passages? (The familiar hymn, "City of God, how broad and far" (E.H. 375), might also be considered.)

2. Consider the medieval idea of Christendom as a Rule of Christ on earth realizable in and through Church and State in co-operation. Contrast with this modern ideas of government.

3. If possible, read part of Mr T. S. Eliot's *Murder in the Cathedral*. (There is no need to discuss the history of the quarrel, though a convenient summary will be found in K. Feiling's *A Hist. of Eng.*, pp. 130–3.) The following sections might be read: from the opening to the entrance of the archbishop, the encounters with the First and Fourth Tempters, the sermon (Becket did preach from the text "Glory to God in the highest, and on earth peace, good will towards men" in his Cathedral on Christmas Day, 1170), and the argument with the Four Knights, concluding with the murder. (Becket was canonized three years after his death.)

Chapter 16

1. Visit a cathedral or abbey or other great medieval church.

2. Show a film or film-strip of a pilgrimage to a cathedral, such as the S.P.C.K. film-strip, *A Pilgrimage to Canterbury Cathedral*. (Many English cathedrals are now in this series.)

3. Describe the house and household of a medieval English rector, and say how he employed his time.

Chapter 17

1. Imagine you are living in the thirteenth century. A friar is preaching in your parish for the first time, in your church. Describe the scene and give your impression.

2. What was the difference between monks and friars?

3. "One cannot help regarding the Crusades as the greatest tragedy in the history of Christianity, and the greatest set-back to the progress of Christ's kingdom on earth" (L. E. Browne, *The Eclipse of Christianity in Asia*, p. 144). (It was not that all the Crusaders were wicked; the best were so wholly mistaken.) Do you think that this verdict is justified?

Chapter 18

1. Secure, if possible, the co-operation of the church organist and demonstrate the plain-song melodies.

2. Study some of the hymns which are translations of the Latin hymns of the Middle Ages. Notice their objective quality. Make a note of the chief medieval hymn-writers. (The Historical ed. of *Hymns Ancient and Modern* can be consulted with advantage on hymns of all periods.)

3. Read extracts from a modern version of *Piers Plowman*. Mr N. Coghill's *Visions from Piers Plowman* is suitable, or there is a rendering in the *Everyman* series. Extracts from what Mr Coghill calls "The Vision of the Coming of Piers Plowman", "The Vision of the World at Work", and "The Vision of the Pardon sent by Truth" (in *Everyman*, "The Vision of the Search for Truth", "The Vision of Piers Counsel" and "The Vision of God's Bull of Pardon") are suggested. All of these illustrate *Do-Well* the active life of honest toil.

4. Read a mystery play, or, better still, see one. A recension of *The York Cycle of Mystery Plays*, made by Dr J. S. Purvis for Mr Martin Browne's production at St Mary's Abbey, York, has been published by S.P.C.K. at 7*s*. 6*d*.

Chapter 19

1. Make a list of some of the ways in which those who could not read could have learnt the faith in the Middle Ages.

2. "It was through the exaltation of the Mother and the Child that innocence and purity came to be reverenced, that women acquired a new dignity and children a right to protection" (H. Maynard Smith, *Pre-Reformation England*, p. 159). Discuss the benefits derived from devotion to the Blessed Virgin by Western Christendom. Compare and contrast this with to-day.

3. How did the Avignon Papacy, the Great Schism and the Conciliar Movement all pave the way for the Reformation?

Chapter 20

1. Write an essay on Martin Luther.

2. Discuss the part played by the printing-press in forwarding the Reformation. (Cf. "Printing is God's latest and best work to

spread the true religion throughout the world" (Luther, *Table Talk*).
Luther is said to have written a book or a pamphlet every fortnight
for over twenty-five years.)

3. What is Justification by Faith? Does the doctrine of Justification by Faith *only* make a visible, institutional Church unnecessary
to the living of the true Christian life? Carlstadt and a few Reformers
said Yes. Most Reformers (including Luther) said No. Which were
right? Discuss.

Chapter 21

1. Colour an outline map of Europe showing (a) the Lutheran
lands; (b) those where the Reformed Church became established or
was permitted; (c) those remaining Roman Catholic.

> Lutheran—Germany (except Bavaria and an area east of the
> Rhine, which remained Roman Catholic), the Baltic States
> and Finland, and the Scandinavian countries including
> Denmark.
> Reformed—Holland, Switzerland, Scotland, a considerable
> district of Germany around Mainz, parts of France.
> Roman Catholic—Italy, Spain, France, Austria, Hungary,
> Poland, Bohemia and Moravia (Czecho-Slovakia), Bel-
> gium, Ireland.

Put bars of the colour representing the Reformed Church across
France. A colour might be selected to represent the Anabaptists,
and some bars of this colour placed across northern Italy, Austria,
Poland, Czecho-Slovakia.

England can be given a colour of its own to represent Anglicanism.

(The folded map in Lindsay, *Hist. of the Reformation*, vol. ii,
would be a useful guide here.)

2. Study the Prayer Book Catechism from "Why was the Sacrament of the Lord's Supper ordained?" to the end. (i) What views of
the Sacramental Presence does the Catechism cover? (It should not
be forgotten that—to quote the late Canon Quick—"there have
always been those who have sought to assert the fact of the Real
Presence without committing themselves to any theory of its manner".) (ii) Taking "remembrance" as meaning "to remember before
God", is the Catechism in line with the teaching of 1 Cor. 11. 26,
and Dr Bright's hymn, "And now, O Father, mindful of the love"
about the sacrificial aspect of the Eucharist?

Chapter 22

1. How would you meet the assertion that the Church of England
was founded by Henry VIII? (It will be clear from the chapter that
Henry did not regard himself as its founder, but the position of the
Church of England *vis-à-vis* Rome needs to be considered in the light
of the relation to Rome of other Churches, such as those of North

Africa, in the early centuries (briefly touched on in ch. 14), and of what has been said in ch. 15. See the pamphlet *Infallible Fallacies*, pp. 15 sqq.)

2. Was Henry's action in dissolving the monasteries justified? Who gained and who lost by the Dissolution?

Index to Volume I

Index